OUR SYRIA

RECIPES from HOME

Itab Azzam and
Dina Mousawi

RUNNING PRESS
PHILADELPHIA

Running Press
Hachette Book Group
1290 Avenue of the Americas, New York, NY 10104
www.runningpress.com
@Running_Press

Printed in China

Originally published in hardcover and ebook by Trapeze, an imprint of The Orion Publishing Group Ltd in May 2017

First U.S. Edition: September 2017

Published by Running Press, an imprint of Perseus Books, LLC, a subsidiary of Hachette Book Group, Inc.

The Hachette Speakers Bureau provides a wide range of authors for speaking events. To find out more, go to www.hachettespeakersbureau.com or call (866) 376-6591.

The publisher is not responsible for websites (or their content) that are not owned by the publisher.

Photography by Liz and Max Haarala Hamilton

Additional photography: Pages 87, 151, 19: Hassan Kattan; pages 48, 49, 50, 51, 102, 121: Susannah Baker-Smith; pages 6, 128: Tabitha Ross

Print book interior design by Steve Marking and Corinda Cook

Library of Congress Control Number: 2017939301

ISBNs: 978-0-7624-9052-3 (hardcover), 978-0-7624-9053-0 (ebook)

1010

10 9 8 7 6 5 4 3 2 1

Contents

Introduction

Since the eighth century BC, for Asians Syria has been the first glimpse of "the Great Sea," a great land of culture to the West, as well as home to the most beautiful ancient mosques and churches. To Westerners, Damascus and Aleppo have always been the gateways to the Orient, the ancient marble and tile work peeking out along tumbledown medieval streets a reminder of the country's biblical and classical heritage. Both of these groups of visitors brought travelers and traders; one bringing pepper, saffron, silk, and porcelain, the other precious metals and new-fangled technology. The markets of Syria still reek of the mingling odors of flowers, spices, tea, baking bread, and its legendary courtyard houses. Both have also brought armies; Tiglath-Pileser's Imperial Army of Assyria, the hoplites of Alexander the Great, crusading knights, Mongol warriors, and Ottoman janissaries have all raped and burned across Syria. Many Syrians alive today were born under French rule. And now, once again, fighters are coming from afar and tearing the country apart.

Our culture is under attack as never before—our greatest buildings are being razed to the ground and our people are fleeing their homeland, disappearing into countries around the globe to seek a new, safer life. But one part of our heritage is still alive and well and will continue no matter what drives families from their homes. This is possibly the country's darkest hour, but even now in tiny flats in Beirut, Berlin, and Bradford, Syrian families are searching out the best tomatoes and lemons, pomegranates and parsley, to recreate the dishes that remind them of home.

Syrians are masters of adversity, and nothing unites and inspires them as much as food. They will let loose with sugar, caffeine, herbs, and spices. A Syrian mother with barely two pennies to rub together can miraculously produce six or seven dishes bursting with flavor every day. And it's an all-day operation—rolling vine leaves, frying huge batches of eggplant, finely chopping parsley for tabbouleh. Such is the power that food has to connect us to our past: we hope that this book will be a way to preserve that hugely rich part of Syrian culture, at a time when it is most at threat.

Itab

When I was growing up in Syria, no one went abroad. My family and I lived in a one-story house that my dad built in a village in the Hauran, the remote and unglamorous mountain region on Syria's border with Jordan—all red soil and black stones—whose main claim to fame over the years has been as a hiding place for rebels and heretics.

We grew up behind the Iron Curtain under Hafez al-Assad, so we missed out on the consumer revolution that took the West by storm in the last century. Even now, everything is cooked fresh. Away from the hurly-burly of the world economy, Syrians have always made their own cheese and yogurt, grown their own olives for olive oil and roses for rose water. The more perspective I get from spending time out of my country, the more extraordinarily vibrant our food culture seems.

We don't stint on flavor. Sweets are very, very sweet; we ladle on the lemon and the pomegranate molasses. And look away now if you don't like raw garlic. Syrians are food chauvinists; nothing elsewhere tastes quite like the flavors of your own village, the way your own mother cooked them. As the last of my family contemplate leaving behind our little village, this is my Noah's ark: a capsule containing the intoxicating taste of home.

Dina

Growing up in Baghdad meant a constant gathering of my huge Iraqi family and, of course, that meant huge feasts to go with it. My dad particularly loved cooking and hosting; naturally my three siblings and I grew up with a passion for food.

Most of my family fled Baghdad during the Iraq War and are now spread all over the world. Many of them are in Amman, and when I visit, I spend every day in a different auntie's kitchen, learning each one's special recipes. What I find interesting is that all my aunties cook the same dish but in a different way, each with her own special ingredient or method. Now I know whose Timan Baagila (fava bean and dill rice) is the most flavorful, whose kebabs are the most succulent, and whose dolma (stuffed vine leaves) are so juicy that I simply cannot stop eating. I have come to realize this is the same with Syrian women too; each has her own special way of making a traditional dish.

My introduction to Syrian cuisine came in 2010, when I was visiting Damascus to research a theater piece I was writing. Waking up to the smell of freshly baked mana'eesh (pizza-like dough with toppings of za'atar, cheese, or meat) and hopping across the road to buy a couple for breakfast was one of my favorite times of day. I soon began to realize just how utterly delicious and flavorful Syrian food is. There are many similarities to Iraqi food, of course, but discovering the intricate flavors of Syrian cuisine added a whole new dimension to my palate.

Dina and Itab

We first met at a friend's house in east London in 2014; we instantly bonded over our mutual love of food—both making and eating it—and we swapped recipes. Since then we have been firm friends, calling each other almost every day to swap tips on our favorite foods.

Later that year, we spent three months together in Beirut, where we reveled in the opportunity to share and refine our recipes. We had gone there to work on a theater project with a large group of Syrian women. We had both been working in Britain for the previous few years, so it was a revelatory experience for us to get back to our roots. Spending day after day with women who'd only recently escaped the war, we discovered what was special about each individual, and we found that as well as resilience, a love of singing, jokes, and stories, all the women we worked with had another common ground: food.

Most days we would receive invites to their homes. They were tiny, shabby little flats to the untrained eye, but to us they were Aladdin's caves of culinary treasures. We heard all the old stories and tasted their wonderfully traditional home cooking. Learning from Fedwa how to scoop a mouthful of tabbouleh with a lettuce leaf rather than a spoon was one memorable quirk of our day; Israa' introducing us to her family tradition of smoked rice was another; as was

Mona teaching us how she relaxed and forgot her worries by making milk pudding.

That's when we hit upon the idea for this book—to bring to the world the glories of Syrian food and in the process honor these brave women who are fighting back against the destruction of their home with the only weapons they have: pots and pans. We desperately wanted to share their great recipes and our love of Syrian food and, to celebrate what food can mean to an individual, to a family, and to a nation.

When we asked thirty-one-year-old Mona how she felt about this book, she replied, "The thought that someone might be cooking my maqloubeh recipe makes me so happy. It means people in the West are thinking of us."

And here we are, two food fanatics who love to share recipes and delicious Syrian dishes. We traveled across Europe and the Middle East, where we met women who welcomed us with humbling generosity, whether they lived in a tent, a rented room, or an apartment. Their stories are the beating heart of this book, and their recipes invite you into their culture with arms wide open.

So forget what you think of when someone mentions Syria today. Let's celebrate what this wonderfully rich, beautiful country does best. Let's eat!

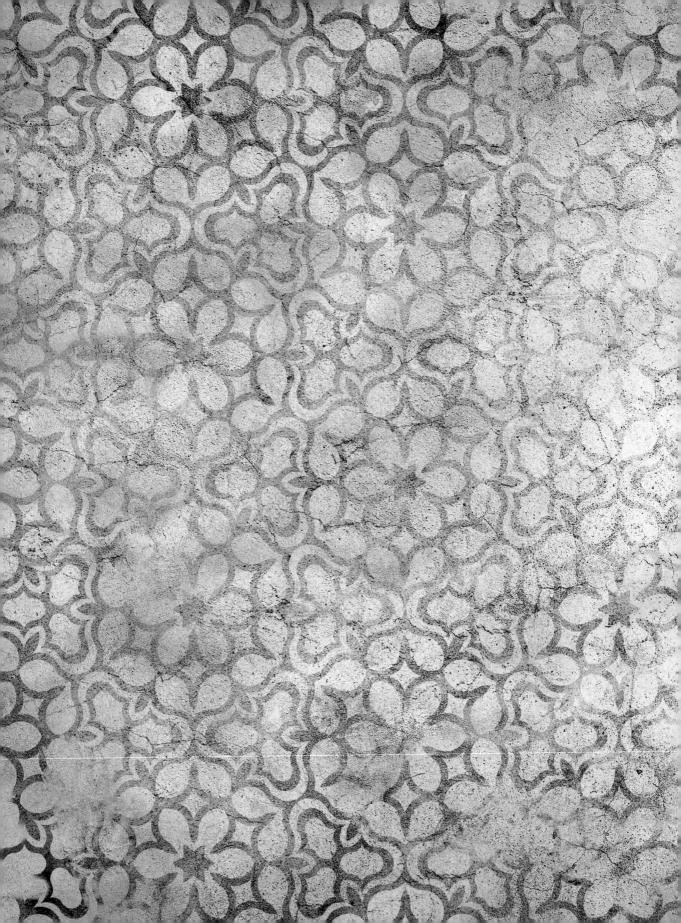

Mezze

Dips and mezze dishes are the bedrock of Syrian cuisine. *Mezze* is an Arabic word that stems from the verb *tamezmez*, which means to enjoy something so much that you savor it slowly.

The question isn't so much *when* do Syrians eat mezze, as when do they not? If you go to someone's house in Syria, there's no way you'll skip the mezze on your way to the main course. We're not talking starters here; these dishes might start to arrive before the bigger meat or rice ones, but they're just as much the focus as what comes later. Cooking a single main course is pretty much unheard of. A proper meal consists of loads of dishes that you all dive into armed with pieces of freshly baked bread between thumb and forefinger. Any vegetable can become part of the mezze. With a bit of garlic, some parsley, or a dash of cumin, the humble, pious runner bean or cauliflower is transformed into a proper treat. Kids don't have to be forced to eat their greens in Syria.

Zucchini in Tahini Sauce

(Mutabal Kusa)

If you are a fan of tahini, this dish is a winner and a nice change from the better-known eggplant mutabal or baba ganoush. In Syria we generally use the small, pale green zucchini that you find all over the Middle East and in a lot of Arab or Turkish markets in Europe, but you can make it just as well with any of the other varieties out there. We've also found this works as a great smoky relish in a ham or cheese sandwich.

You can serve this in two different ways: either pour the Tahini Sauce on top of the zucchini rounds, or mash up the zucchini using a fork and mix them with the sauce, to make a dip. Either way, it is delicious with a sprinkling of dried mint and sumac on top.

SERVES 4 AS PART OF A MEZZE

5 baby zucchini, sliced into ¼-inch/½ cm rounds

Vegetable oil, for frying

Salt, to taste

3 tablespoons Tahini Sauce (page 243)

Sumac, to taste

Dried mint, to taste

Fry the zucchini on both sides in a generous amount of oil. When they are brown and crispy, place on a paper towel to soak up any excess oil. Season with salt.

Mash the zucchini, if you like, and mix together with the Tahini Sauce if you are making a dip, or drizzle the sauce on top of the zucchini rounds. Sprinkle with sumac and dried mint.

Eggplant Fetteh

(Fetteh Beitinjaan)

Layering food on toasted bread with a yogurt sauce is a distinctly Syrian specialty. As far as Syrians are concerned, no flavor has yet been found that can't be enhanced by the addition of garlicky yogurt and a bit of crunch.

Bread is considered a sacred gift from God in the Arab world, whether you are Muslim, Druze, or Christian, and it's a sin to waste it even after it has gone stale. That's one of the reasons why *fetteh*—literally, "breadcrumbs"—is such a popular dish and can be made with chickpeas, eggplant, chicken, or lamb. Whenever we make Eggplant Fetteh for friends it is always everyone's favorite dish on the table.

SERVES 4 AS PART OF A MEZZE

3 medium eggplants

Olive oil, for roasting and drizzling

Salt, to taste

2 flatbreads or pitas

2 cups/500 g plain yogurt

2 small garlic cloves, crushed

2 tablespoons lemon juice

Handful of roughly chopped parsley

Handful of pomegranate seeds

½ cup/50 g toasted pine nuts

Heat the oven to 350°F/180°C.

Cut the eggplants into quarters lengthwise and then slice them into ½-inch/1 cm chunks and place on a baking tray. Pour over a generous helping of olive oil and a sprinkle of salt, then roast in the oven for approximately 40 minutes, or until the eggplant is soft.

Brush the bread with olive oil and toast in the oven for about 10 minutes until nice and crispy. Then break it up into pieces.

In a bowl combine the yogurt, garlic, and lemon juice.

When the eggplants are ready, take them out of the oven and allow to cool. Place them in a shallow bowl, then pour the yogurt mixture on top.

When ready to serve, season to taste, sprinkle with the crispy bread, parsley, pomegranate seeds, and toasted pine nuts.

Red Pepper and Walnut Dip

(Mhammara)

Traditionally from Aleppo, this sophisticated hot red pepper dip has traveled all over the Levant. *Mhammara* means "roasted until red," which gives just the right sense of its earthy, fiery flavor. The color comes from the roasted red peppers, but the real key is the walnuts, which are everywhere in Syria. This is possibly our favorite of Syria's myriad walnut dishes.

Everyone has their own way of making it, and we tried more versions than we can remember on our travels—from scorching hot to sweet and crunchy. Most people use breadcrumbs or bulgur, but we found that you don't actually need either.

SERVES 4–6 AS PART OF A MEZZE

2 red bell peppers or 7-ounce/200 g jar of chargrilled peppers

1 red cayenne or birdseye chile

¾ cup/75 g walnuts, toasted

1 teaspoon red pepper paste (page 242), hot or medium

1 garlic clove

1 tablespoon pomegranate molasses

3 tablespoons olive oil, plus extra for drizzling

Salt and pepper, to taste

Flatbreads, to serve

For fresh peppers, preheat the oven to 350°F/180°C. Cut the pepper and chile in half and remove the cores and seeds. Place on a baking tray skin-side up, drizzle with olive oil and salt, then roast in the oven until they soften and darken, 15 to 20 minutes.

If using jarred peppers, and combine with the charred and cooled chile.

Blend the walnuts in a food processor until chopped, then add the pepper, chile, red pepper paste, garlic, molasses, olive oil, and salt and pepper and blend well.

Drizzle with olive oil and serve with flatbreads.

Beet Dip
(Mutabal Shwandar)

Not traditionally a Syrian mezze dish, this beet dip has been around in Lebanon for many years and has since traveled the Levant, making its way into many Damascene restaurants. We love its rich color, which brightens up any table. Roasting the beets creates a thicker, darker dip, but if you don't have time to roast them, using ready-cooked boiled ones is also fine.

SERVES 4–6 AS PART OF A MEZZE

4 medium beets
Olive oil, for roasting and drizzling
Salt and pepper, to taste
2 tablespoons tahini
2 tablespoons plain yogurt
1 garlic clove, crushed
Juice of ½ lemon
Chopped parsley, to garnish

Heat the oven to 350°F/180°C.

Scrub the beets well, trim the edges, and slice into wedges. Place in a baking tray, pour over a generous helping of olive oil, and season with salt and pepper. Roast for around 30 minutes, or until they are soft enough so that a sharp knife can easily be inserted all the way through. Take out of the oven and leave to cool.

Blend the beets in a food processor with tahini, yogurt, garlic, and lemon juice, until you have a smooth, pinky-purple-colored dip. Season to taste.

Drizzle with olive oil and sprinkle with parsley for a lovely clash of purple and green.

Roasted Cauliflower with Cumin

(Zahra wa Kamoon)

Cauliflower is used a lot in Syrian home cooking, partly because it is so cheap. On its own it is a little bland, but Syrians have managed to find combinations that elevate the humble cauliflower to the level of a delicacy.

This is a great dish for vegans; you can either serve this as part of a mezze or as a side dish. It also goes well with any of our fish recipes.

This roasted cauliflower can be eaten warm or cold, but if you do roast it in advance, pour the dressing over at the last minute to prevent the cauliflower from becoming soggy. You can roast the spines of the leaves with the cauliflower to add a bit of color and texture. Another option is to drizzle Tahini Sauce over the dish (see page 243).

SERVES 4 AS PART OF A MEZZE

1 large whole cauliflower, chopped into florets

Vegetable oil, for roasting

Salt and pepper, to taste

For the dressing

1 garlic clove

¼ teaspoon sea salt

3 tablespoons/45 ml extra-virgin olive oil

Juice of ½ lemon

½ teaspoon ground cumin

Small handful of chopped parsley

Handful of toasted pine nuts or almonds

Salt and pepper, to taste

Heat the oven to 350°F/180°C.

Roast the cauliflower florets with a little vegetable oil, salt, and pepper for around 30 minutes, or until they have turned golden brown.

While the cauliflower is cooking, make the dressing by crushing the garlic and salt with a pestle and mortar, adding the olive oil, lemon juice, and cumin, and whisking everything together. Season with salt and pepper.

Pour the dressing over the roasted cauliflower and sprinkle with parsley and almonds to serve.

Red Lentil Kibbeh

(Kibbeh Addas)

"Bulgur is coral but lentils are pearls" is a common saying in northern Aleppo, where lentils are widely cultivated. There are some village names that even have the word "lentil" in them, such as Yaked Al Adas (Yaked of the Lentils).

These vegan red lentil kibbeh do tend to dry out if not eaten fairly quickly, but they are so delicious we find it rarely proves to be a problem.

MAKES 14 KIBBEH

For the kibbeh

½ heaped cup/100 g red lentils

2 cups/500 ml water

1 onion, finely chopped

3 tablespoons vegetable oil

¼ cup/40 g fine bulgur wheat

Salt, to taste

¼ cup/4 tablespoons olive oil

1 tablespoon finely chopped mint

1 tablespoon finely chopped parsley

½ teaspoon red pepper paste (page 242)

½ teaspoon ground cumin

¼ teaspoon Aleppo pepper

For the salsa

12 cherry tomatoes, finely diced

1 green bell pepper, seeded and finely diced

1 small onion, very finely diced

2 tablespoons pomegranate seeds

1 tablespoon olive oil

1 tablespoon pomegranate molasses

Juice of 1 lemon

Salt, to taste

Rinse and drain the bulgur and leave to one side. Rinse the lentils, then in a saucepan, bring the lentils and water to a boil and cook at a simmer until almost all the liquid has evaporated. Stir regularly.

Meanwhile, over a very low heat gently fry the onion in the vegetable oil for about 30 minutes until caramelized.

Once the water from the lentils is almost all gone, add the bulgur and salt and keep simmering until the water has completely evaporated and the lentil mixture has made a thick paste.

Meanwhile, mix all the ingredients for the salsa together in a bowl. Add more salt or lemon juice to taste.

When the lentils and bulgur are completely dry, like the texture of mashed potatoes, take off the heat and stir in the olive oil, mint, parsley, red pepper paste, cumin, Aleppo pepper, and caramelized onions. Leave the mixture until it is cool enough to handle then make into little oval-shaped patties with your hands.

Serve with the salsa.

Spinach Kibbeh

(Kibbeh Zankaliyeh)

Kibbeh Zankaliyeh is one of the more unusual versions of kibbeh: it is completely vegan, not deep-fried, and the preparation time is relatively quick. It makes an excellent starter as well as great finger food, drizzled with pomegranate molasses and served with a bit of yogurt on the side. It's also surprisingly good eaten cold the next day, and makes the perfect lunch box filler.

MAKES 15–18 PIECES

⅔ cup/100 g fine bulgur wheat

10 ounces/300 g spinach, coarsely chopped

Handful of finely chopped parsley

Handful of finely chopped cilantro

4 spring onions, chopped

⅔ cup/100 g cooked chickpeas, roughly mashed

1 teaspoon ground cumin

1 teaspoon salt

1 teaspoon black pepper

1 teaspoon Aleppo pepper

1 teaspoon 7 spices (page 244)

2 to 3 garlic cloves, crushed

⅔ cup/100 g all-purpose flour

½ teaspoon baking powder

2 tablespoons vegetable oil, plus extra for frying

Pomegranate molasses, to serve

Plain yogurt, to serve

Rinse the bulgur a couple of times, then leave to one side to drain completely.

Place the bulgur and all the remaining ingredients in a large mixing bowl and knead well with your hands. The spinach will break up and the whole mixture will eventually have a paste-like consistency. Cover and leave in the fridge for 20 to 30 minutes.

When you are ready to make the kibbeh, take a small bit of the mix, knead it in your hands and roll into a ball, then flatten it out using the palms of both hands to form a disc shape. Place on a plate until you have finished all the mix. You may have to wash your hands after every few kibbeh as they will get sticky.

Heat some vegetable oil in a frying pan and shallow-fry the kibbeh for about 2 minutes on each side, until they are lightly browned, taking care not to overcook them. You may need to do this in batches. Remove the kibbeh from the pan with a spatula and place on paper towels until you are ready to serve.

Drizzle the kibbeh with pomegranate molasses and serve with a helping of plain yogurt on the side.

Hummus with Meat
(Hummus bi Lahmi)

Hummus has come to epitomize Middle Eastern cuisine for most Westerners. The word *hummus* literally means "chickpeas" in Arabic. "Hummus bi Tahina" is the proper name for the dip we all know and goes back at least to the time of the Crusades; the oldest recipe we could find for "Hummus with Tahini Sauce" appeared in a thirteenth-century Arabic cookbook. Some people say that the great Saladin himself used to prepare his own version.

Such is its celebrity status in the food world that in recent years hummus has become politicized, with countries across the Mediterranean each pressing their own claim of ownership over it. But as a Syrian and an Iraqi we'd like to remind you that chickpeas were first cultivated in Mesopotamia (ancient Iraq and Syria). We'll leave the final judgment to you. The authentic way to make this recipe is to boil dried chickpeas, and it's worth it, as the hummus will have a much smoother texture.

SERVES 4 AS PART OF A MEZZE

For the hummus

1 cup/150 g dried chickpeas (soaked overnight in water with ¼ teaspoon baking soda), or 1 (14-ounce/400 g) can chickpeas

1 garlic clove, crushed

1 generous tablespoon tahini

Juice of 1 lemon

Salt and pepper, to taste

For the topping

7 ounces/200 g boneless leg of lamb, diced (substitute ground lamb)

Vegetable oil, for frying

Salt and pepper, to taste

Handful of pine nuts, toasted

Extra-virgin olive oil, to serve

Flatbreads, to serve

Drain the chickpeas, then cover with lots of fresh water and boil for 2 hours until tender, if using the dried ones. Save the cooking water or the water in the can for later. Pick out any loose chickpea skins and then blend really well in a food processor with the garlic, tahini, lemon juice, salt and pepper, and 7 tablespoons of cooking water. If it looks a bit dry, add some more water gradually, just enough not to overdilute. It should be very smooth.

Fry the meat in a frying pan over high heat with a little oil, until it browns, then season with salt and pepper.

Using the back of a spoon spread the hummus in a shallow bowl. Scatter the meat and pine nuts on top and add a drizzle of olive oil. Serve with flatbreads.

Smoked Eggplant Salad

(Mkhabasa)

We were given this recipe by Majdoleen from Dara'a; she was very shy and quiet when we worked with her in a theater workshop, but a confident, natural leader in the kitchen. We first realized this when she invited us into her home in the Shatila camp in Beirut, to teach us some of her specialties, and to our surprise she turned out to be both a fantastic cook and a forceful character. We spent a couple of days cooking with her, her three friends, and her fourteen-year-old daughter, who was eagerly watching everything to pick up her mother's skills.

The name *Mkhabasa* derives from the word *mkhabas*, which means "busy," and is so named because, as Majdoleen said, "the dish is a crazy mix of ingredients and colors so it looks busy." We also think it's a great starter to whip up when you are in a rush, because it's so quick to make, yet utterly healthy and delicious.

SERVES 4 AS PART OF A MEZZE

2 medium eggplants

Handful of parsley, finely chopped

¼ each, red, yellow, and green bell peppers, seeded and finely diced

1 tomato, diced

Handful of walnuts, coarsely chopped

2 tablespoons pomegranate molasses

Juice of ½ lemon

Salt and pepper, to taste

Extra-virgin olive oil, to serve

Place the eggplants over an open flame and grill or broil, turning regularly so that the whole eggplant is charred and wilted. Put in a colander and leave to cool before peeling.

Once peeled, place the eggplant flesh in a bowl, mash with a fork, and add the parsley, peppers, tomato, walnuts, molasses, lemon juice, and salt and pepper. Mix everything together, season with more salt and pepper as needed, and drizzle with olive oil. It couldn't be easier.

Fava Beans with Cilantro and Garlic

(Ful wa Kuzbara)

This recipe uses frozen green fava beans instead of the widely used dried brown ones. As a side dish, it goes beautifully with fish but it's also great on its own or spooned over toast with a bit of yogurt dolloped on top. There is also a variation that makes a great breakfast, in which you simply add fried eggs.

SERVES 4 AS PART OF A MEZZE

Vegetable oil, for frying

1 (14-ounce/400 g) bag frozen fava beans, defrosted

2 to 3 garlic cloves, finely chopped

Handful of chopped cilantro

Salt and pepper, to taste

Extra-virgin olive oil, for drizzling

Juice of ½ lemon (optional)

Heat a bit of vegetable oil in a frying pan, add the beans, and cook over low heat until they have softened, then add the garlic. After a couple of minutes throw in the cilantro and stir, then take off the heat, season, and drizzle with olive oil. Squeeze lemon juice over the beans for extra zing, if you like.

Zucchini with Garlic and Mint

(Kusa wa Na'na)

This recipe is a popular response to the Syrian horror of wasting food. Stuffed zucchini is a very popular dish in Syria, but that leaves the question of what to do with the flesh that you scoop out. Here is the answer, and it has become so popular that people no longer wait until they have leftover zucchini from kusa mahshi (stuffed zucchini); they've now started making it with whole zucchinis, peeled, diced, and cooked in a tomato sauce, rather than just served with mint and garlic.

SERVES 4 AS PART OF A MEZZE

Vegetable oil, for frying

Scooped-out 6 baby zucchini or 2 large whole zucchini, peeled and diced

3 to 4 garlic cloves, crushed

Salt and pepper, to taste

Dried mint, to taste

Extra-virgin olive oil, for drizzling

Flatbread, to serve

Heat a bit of oil in a frying pan, then add the zucchini and fry over low heat for 5 to 10 minutes until they soften. Add the garlic and fry for a few more minutes. Season with salt, pepper, and dried mint to taste.

Drizzle with extra-virgin olive oil and serve with flatbread.

Stuffed Vine Leaves
(Yulangi)

Quite a few of the women we worked with made us these stuffed vine leaves, which are a very popular addition to a mezze. Every woman told us what her own special little secret was, and as we went from home to home, we discovered that everyone's special secret is the same: add a teaspoon of ground cardamom coffee into the rice mixture to give it the cardamom flavor. We experimented by adding ground cardamom without the coffee, and it actually tastes the same.

Ideally, you should use fresh vine leaves to make yulangi, but you might have a hard time finding them. Any Arabic or Turkish supermarket will sell you the preserved ones that come in a jar or vacuum packed.

These stuffed leaves may seem difficult to make from scratch, but they're actually quite straightforward, once you get the hang of rolling them. When rolled, do make sure they are tightly packed in the pan to avoid them coming loose.

3 tomatoes

2 onions

2 to 3 potatoes, peeled

1¼ cups/250 g short-grain rice, rinsed and drained well

4 tablespoons olive oil, plus extra for drizzling

Handful of chopped fresh mint

Handful of chopped fresh cilantro

Handful of chopped fresh parsley

1 teaspoon salt

1 teaspoon 7 spices (page 244)

½ teaspoon ground cardamom

Juice of 1 lemon, plus extra half for squeezing

1(15-ounce/425 g) jar preserved vine leaves, drained and rinsed

Cut 1 tomato, 1 onion, and all the potatoes into ½-inch/1 cm-thick slices and layer them at the bottom of a large saucepan.

Finely dice the second onion, seed and finely dice the remaining tomatoes, and place them in a bowl with the rice, oil, herbs, salt, 7 spices, cardamom, and lemon juice and mix well.

Now take a vine leaf, making sure the rough side is facing up, the leaf is spread out flat, and the center point is nearest to you. Place about a teaspoon of the rice mixture at the bottom, in a horizontal line. Don't overfill, as the rice will expand when cooked. Roll the vine leaf into a long, thin finger shape, tucking the sides in and ensuring the rice mixture is tightly wrapped. The quantities here allow for a few broken leaves and messed-up rolls.

Place each neatly rolled vine leaf in the saucepan next to another one tightly. The less space between them, the less moving around. Every couple of layers, pour on a tablespoon of olive oil. Once you have used up either all the leaves or all the rice, you are ready to cook. Place any leftover leaves flat over the stuffed ones and put a weighted plate or lid directly on top of the rolls.

Turn the heat on the stovetop to medium-high and cook the leaves for about 5 minutes, then pour boiling water over the vine leaves so that the water is about ½ inch/1 cm above the weighted plate. Bring to a rapid boil over high heat, then lower the heat and simmer, covered, for about 1½ hours. When all the water has evaporated, test a roll, and if it's not cooked, add more water and keep simmering.

When the rice is tender, squeeze half a lemon over the vine leaves and leave to rest for 5 minutes or so. Remove the stuffed vine leaves from the pan, either by placing a large tray on top and flipping it over, or one by one, not forgetting the potatoes, tomato, and onion at the bottom of the pan, which will be full of flavor by now. Drizzle a little more olive oil over the rolls and serve immediately, or chill and serve as part of a cold mezze.

Charred Eggplant Dip
(Mutabal)

There is some confusion over the name of this delicious smoky dip. Most people in the West know it as baba ganoush, and, indeed, in Iraq people do call it that; but in Syria, Lebanon, and Jordan, baba ganoush is a different dish, more like the salad on page 32, and this dip is called *Mutabal*, which means "spiced." Strictly speaking you can call any vegetable dip "mutabal"; you can have zucchini or beet mutabal, for example.

Charring the eggplants is the secret to this dip and is what gives it its unique taste. Most people do this directly over an open flame on their gas stovetop, but you can grill or broil them if you don't have gas. It may sound like a hassle to char your eggplants, but it is actually super easy and only takes about 10 minutes. It does help to have a pair of tongs, though!

SERVES 4 AS PART OF A MEZZE

2 medium eggplants

1 garlic clove

Salt, to taste

3 tablespoons plain yogurt

2 tablespoons tahini

Juice of 1 lemon

Olive oil, for drizzling

Handful of pomegranate seeds, to serve (optional)

Flatbread, to serve

Using a sharp knife, pierce the eggplants about ¾ inch/ 2 cm deep and place them over an open flame (or cook them under a preheated broiler). Turn occasionally to make sure each side blackens evenly. After about 10 minutes (depending on the size of the eggplants), they will begin to wilt and spit.

Once the eggplants are completely wilted and the skin is charred and crispy, remove from the flame. Holding the green top with one hand and a sharp knife in the other, gently peel the thin layer of burnt skin off, cut away the green top, and discard both. Transfer the flesh to a bowl and leave to one side.

Crush the garlic and salt with a pestle and mortar.

Using a fork, mash the eggplant flesh, add the garlic paste, and stir well. Then add the rest of the ingredients and mix.

Serve drizzled with olive oil and sprinkled with pomegranate seeds, if you like, with some bread alongside.

Green Beans in Olive Oil

(Lubiyeh bil Zeit)

We love this dish; it's fresh, simple, and complements a feast full of more elaborate dishes. Don't get us wrong: these beans taste delicious, but they're just not quite as rich as some of the other recipes. You can either use fine green beans or flat runner beans, which are better cut diagonally, or at least, that seems to be how every Syrian woman we met prepares them.

This would be served as a side or as part of a mezze, but if you wanted to serve beans as a main course, there is another commonly used recipe for green beans in tomato sauce that you can find on page 119.

SERVES 2–4 AS A SIDE DISH

1 pound/450 g green beans, edges trimmed off and cut in half

Vegetable oil, for frying

4 garlic cloves, crushed

Salt, to taste

Handful of fresh cilantro, chopped

Extra-virgin olive oil, to serve

In a frying pan, sauté the beans in a bit of vegetable oil for about 5 minutes. Bring a kettle of water to a boil.

Add a little boiling water to the beans and simmer until they soften and all the water has evaporated. You don't want the beans to be totally covered with water, just about ½ inch/1 cm is enough. If the beans are still not cooked, add a bit more water and simmer until they do cook. Lastly add the crushed garlic and salt. Keep on the heat for another minute, then turn off, add the cilantro, and season with more salt to taste. Drizzle with extra-virgin olive oil to serve.

Spicy Potatoes
(Batata Harra)

This is a classic side dish nowadays. It has migrated from people's homes to restaurants, and it's now on the menu, it seems, of almost every restaurant from the Mediterranean to the Euphrates, and you can actually find it in quite a few Arabic restaurants in the UK. It is perfect as part of a mezze, but if you want to mix things up, it also makes a nice variation of roasted potatoes with Sunday dinner.

SERVES 4 AS PART OF A MEZZE

4 medium yellow potatoes, peeled and cut into ¾-inch/2 cm cubes

Olive oil, for roasting

Salt, to taste

3 garlic cloves, finely chopped

2 red cayenne chiles, seeded and finely chopped

1 bunch of cilantro, chopped

1 tablespoon ground Aleppo pepper

Heat the oven to 400°F/200°C.

Roast the potatoes with olive oil and salt for about 30 minutes, or until they are a nice golden brown color.

Meanwhile, quickly fry the garlic, chiles, and half the cilantro until the garlic is golden. Once the potatoes are ready, combine the garlic mixture with the potatoes, Aleppo pepper, and the remaining cilantro.

Chard with Garlic and Lemon

(Assoura)

Every spring most of the women in Itab's home village in Sweida, in southwest Syria, go on daily excursions to pick wild herbs and leaves. Huge numbers of people depend on these natural resources for their daily meals at that time of year, and for weeks all around the countryside, women can be seen moving in big scattered groups, singing, gossiping, drinking maté tea, or picnicking. It is a beautiful ritual with a double purpose, providing nutrition, but more importantly, an excuse to get out of the house without husbands, fathers, or brothers.

All these freshly picked greens are eaten with labneh (thickened yogurt–see page 56), and the leaves are wilted and mixed with good olive oil, garlic, and lemon. It's all perfectly simple, nutritious, and cheap. A lot of the wild herbs and leaves that get picked up, such as mallow leaves, are pretty hard to find in the West, but one is readily available—and that's chard.

Traditionally, people eat this dish simply with a dollop of yogurt and a bit of bread, or you can serve it as a side dish with lamb or chicken.

SERVES 4 AS A SIDE OR PART OF A MEZZE

1 pound/400 g chard or rainbow chard

4 garlic cloves, crushed

Juice of 1 lemon

Extra-virgin olive oil, to serve

Salt, to taste

Wash and coarsely chop the chard, then place it in a large pan over medium heat, without any oil, and leave to wilt with a lid on. The little bit of water on the leaves from washing will help steam them.

Once all the leaves have wilted and the water has evaporated, turn off the heat. Add the garlic and lemon juice and a generous amount of extra-virgin olive oil, season with salt, and serve.

Spinach with Sumac

(Spanekh wa Sumac)

We have made this for several friends, and it's so simple and delicious that we couldn't resist including it in this book. The juxtaposition of the lemony sumac flavor with earthy spinach adds comfort, freshness, and zing. You can have it on its own, or as a topping for puff pastry. We also love it with fish, and it's great both hot and cold.

SERVES 4 AS PART OF A MEZZE

1 small red onion, finely diced or sliced

Olive oil, for frying

12 ounces/350 g baby spinach

1 tablespoon sumac

A squeeze of lemon juice

Salt and pepper, to taste

Pomegranate seeds, to serve (optional)

Plain yogurt and flatbread, to serve

Over very low heat, fry the onion in a little olive oil for 20 to 30 minutes, until softened and almost caramelized. Add the spinach leaves and cook them until wilted. Turn off the heat, then sprinkle on the sumac, a squeeze of lemon, salt and pepper, and stir. Sprinkle the pomegranate seeds over, if using.

Serve with yogurt and bread.

Ramadan and Lent

Ramadan in Damascus is like nothing else. It is magical. Every evening you wait hungrily for the sound of the canon being fired, which gives the all-clear for breaking your fast. Minutes later you're lucky if you see another human being on the streets. It's a mass self-imposed curfew; the only sound in the city's empty alleyways is the distant clink from the spoons of hungry people hitting their plates.

At the crack of dawn you have to listen out for the Musaharati, the wake-up man. This tradition is so rooted in the soul of Damascus that sometimes even Christians do it too. The Musaharati, dressed up in traditional clothes, goes around the alleys beating a drum and singing to people to wake up for the pre-dawn meal, before they start their lengthy fast through the daylight hours. "You who are fasting, wake up to please your immortal God," he calls, then hits a few bangs on the drum before moving on to the next street or alleyway where he repeats it all.

The main event is the evening meal, Iftar, literally "break fast." Dates and juice are absolutely necessary staples for Iftar. A date must be the first thing you eat to break your fast, followed by fruit juice—ideally tamarind (page 228)—the traditional preludes

to a massive binge. The closest Western culture comes to the joy and excitement of Iftar is Christmas dinner, but this is Christmas dinner every night for a month.

Christians in Syria also have their own high days and holidays with their own food traditions. Hala from Damascus (page 86) told us about her childhood memories of creating a delicious boiled-wheat dessert called sleeqa and decorating it with colorful sweets like Smarties and licorice every autumn for Eid St. Barbara. On their name days they would have a party with pastries, tabbouleh, cake, and jelly, and every twenty-fifth of December all the other sects would go and wish the Christian families Happy Christmas and receive a gift of sweets in return.

The Christian fast is, of course, Lent. This is a big deal in Old Damascus, especially in Bab Touma, near where St. Paul famously converted, or in Aramaic villages like Ma'aloula, in the southern uplands of the Hauran or Wadi Nasara, the valley of the Christians near Homs. During Lent, eating meat or dairy products is strictly forbidden, so the festival has helped give birth to Syria's rich tradition of vegan cooking, including signature dishes such as our all-time favorite, Mtabak.

Eggplants with Tomato
(Mtabak)

There is a famous Syrian saying: "If the oil doesn't drip down your elbow when you're eating, the dish isn't tasty enough." This olive-oil-based recipe is one of the dishes we cooked with Hala (page 86), who is Christian, and it's one of the many vegan dishes that Christians eat during Lent in Syria. It is mouthwatering when you cook it and tastes even better the next day.

Hala used canned tomatoes in this dish—partly for convenience but also because she thinks fresh tomatoes in the U.K. aren't reliably tasty. "Don't tell my mother; she'd kill me!" she whispered to us. If you want a healthier option, you can roast the eggplants in the oven. Mtabak is always eaten with green peppers. There are people who cook the peppers in the sauce and some who eat them raw on the side.

SERVES 4 AS PART OF A MEZZE

2 large eggplants, green tops chopped off and skin peeled in strips

Salt, to taste

Olive oil, for frying and drizzling

1 onion, sliced

2 garlic cloves, chopped

7 very ripe large tomatoes, roughly chopped, or 1 (14-ounce/400 g) can chopped tomatoes

2 tablespoons tomato paste

Pinch of granulated sugar

Flatbread and sliced raw green peppers, to serve

Cut the eggplants in half widthways and cut each half into ½-inch/1 cm-thick slices. Salt and set aside for 10 minutes. Pat dry with a paper towel.

Shallow-fry the eggplants in a pan with plenty of olive oil until they soften and turn golden brown, then transfer to a plate lined with paper towels to soak up the oil. Alternatively, you can roast them in an oven heated to 350°F/180°C for 30 to 40 minutes.

In a clean frying pan, fry the onion in olive oil over medium–low heat for 3 to 4 minutes, then add the garlic and fry for a further 3 to 4 minutes. Add the tomatoes, reduce the heat to low, and simmer with the lid on.

After 15 minutes, add the tomato paste, sugar, and salt to taste, and continue to simmer for 30 minutes. When the tomato sauce is dark and thick, add the fried eggplants and simmer for a further 5 minutes.

Pour everything into a shallow bowl and drizzle with olive oil. Serve with flatbread and peppers.

Cabbage and Mint Salad

(Malfouf wa Na'na')

A very popular, quick, cheap, and simple salad that goes with pretty much any meal. We were often served this as part of a big feast at many of the women's houses we visited. If you don't like raw garlic, simply leave it out.

SERVES 4 AS PART OF A MEZZE

1 white cabbage, very finely shredded

1 garlic clove, crushed

Sea salt, to taste

Juice of 1 small lemon

2 tablespoons extra-virgin olive oil

1 tablespoon dried mint

Aleppo pepper flakes, to serve (optional)

Put the shredded cabbage in a large salad bowl.

In a pestle and mortar, smash the garlic with some sea salt until it is a paste, then add the lemon juice and olive oil and whisk together.

Pour the dressing over the cabbage, add the mint, and mix well.

Season with salt and, if you want to add a little kick to it, some Aleppo pepper flakes.

Spiced Olives

(Zeitoun Mutabal)

You can hardly find a Syrian country house without an olive tree or two in the garden.

Most people make their own olive oil and pickle their own olives. Syrians eat them all the time; for breakfast in a wrap with labneh and fresh mint, as a mezze spread, or even just on their own with a bit of olive oil and bread. Spiced olives with herbs could form part of a mezze or be served as nibbles when your guests arrive.

SERVES 2–4 AS PART OF A MEZZE

8 ounces/225 g green pitted olives

1 garlic clove, chopped

Small handful of parsley, finely chopped

½ teaspoon ground cumin

½ teaspoon ground Aleppo pepper

A dash of pomegranate molasses

A squeeze of lemon juice

Mix all the ingredients in a bowl and serve.

Strained Yogurt

(Labneh)

MAKES 14 SMALL BALLS OR 1 CUP/250 ML OF SPREADABLE LABNEH

1 teaspoon salt

2 cups/500 g plain yogurt

Olive oil, to serve

Chopped mint, to serve

Mix the salt with the yogurt. Line a sieve with a cheesecloth and place on top of a bowl. Pour the yogurt into the cheesecloth and fold the cheesecloth over. Place a heavy item on top and leave to strain at room temperature for 24 hours.

The next day, the yogurt should be drained of all liquid and have a nice thick consistency. You can then make this into balls and place in a jar with enough olive oil to cover them. Alternatively, leave in a bowl as a spread, and sprinkle mint on top.

Fresh Thyme and Halloumi Salad
(Salatat Za'atar)

This salad from Aleppo adds a fragrant, citrusy edge to any meal and is possibly our favorite salad recipe in the whole book. It makes for a particularly great combination with roast lamb or roast chicken. The dressing left at the end is great for dipping crusty bread.

The old city of Aleppo in general is famous for its distinctive za'atar, a spice mix made of dried thyme and sesame, which is one of the must-have Syrian cupboard ingredients. It is imperative that if you visit Aleppo you return with a bag of their za'atar as a gift for friends.

SERVES 2 AS A SIDE

0.7 ounces/20 g fresh thyme

3 ½ ounces/100 g halloumi, cut roughly into ½-inch/1 cm cubes

1 tomato, diced

½ small red onion, very thinly sliced

1 teaspoon ground Aleppo pepper

A squeeze of lemon

1 tablespoon pomegranate molasses

Olive oil, for drizzling

Make sure you buy the greenest, freshest thyme that doesn't have woody stalks. Coarsely chop the thyme. If there are any particularly thick stalks, strip the leaves by running your fingers down the length of the stalk from top to bottom. Place the leaves in a bowl.

Add the halloumi, tomato, onion, pepper, lemon juice, and molasses to the bowl and mix well. Drizzle with oil and serve.

Tabbouleh

When we were in Beirut we found a shop selling greeting cards that read:
"You are the parsley to my tabbouleh," which tells you how high tabbouleh
ranks in the Levantine pantheon. You couldn't write a Syrian cookbook
without including it. This salad is beloved by the whole Arab world, and
is one of the few dishes that needs no translation.

Parsley is very rich in vitamin C, and Fedwa (see page 175) told us she makes
it at least once a week. "Tabbouleh is a very important part of our diet,
especially when eating meat dishes, as it provides all the vitamins." In her
family they enjoy scooping up a mouthful of tabbouleh with a lettuce leaf,
and so do we.

SERVES 4 AS PART OF A MEZZE

2 large bunches of parsley

½ bunch of mint

2 tablespoons fine bulgur wheat

**Juice of 1½ lemons and zest
of 1 lemon**

2 spring onions, finely chopped

**2 large tomatoes, seeded
and finely diced**

Extra-virgin olive oil, to serve

Salt, to taste

Rinse the parsley and mint well and leave to dry.

Soak the bulgur in the juice of 1 lemon and set aside while
you prepare the other ingredients.

Chop the parsley and mint very finely and put in a large
mixing bowl. Add the onions, tomato, bulgur with soaking
juice, and the lemon zest and mix well.

Dress with olive oil, the juice of half a lemon, and salt.

Pumpkin Kibbeh

(Kibbeh Kara'aa)

In one of the poshest restaurants in an affluent neighborhood of Beirut, we met Dzovik, a Syrian Armenian lady from Aleppo. Dzovik has been looking after her disabled husband for more than 15 years. Her son, who was conscripted into the Syrian army before the conflict started, is still serving in the military six years on, because the regime refused to release him at the end of his term of duty, even though he had a wife and child. Intense fighting meant Dzovik left her home with her husband, daughter-in-law, and grandson and headed towards the Syrian coast, thinking she would only be away for two weeks or so. Those two weeks have now become four years and have taken her on to Beirut, where she waits for her son to be released from the army. She is now responsible for supporting her entire family, which she does by working as a head chef in one of Beirut's best Armenian restaurants.

These are great with either Tahini Sauce (page 243) or the pomegranate sauce here.

For the dough

1½ pounds/650 g pumpkin
or butternut squash, peeled
and cut up

1 small onion

1⅓ cups/220 g fine bulgur wheat

1 teaspoon salt

1 teaspoon black pepper

¾ cup/120 g all-purpose flour

Vegetable oil, for deep-frying

For the stuffing

1 small yellow onion, peeled
and quartered

Oil, for frying

1½ teaspoons 7 spices (page 244)

1 teaspoon salt

1 teaspoon black pepper

½ teaspoon ground Aleppo pepper

4 to 5 handfuls of baby spinach

¾ cup/100 g cooked chickpeas

4 cups/40 g walnuts, chopped

2 tablespoons pomegranate
molasses (page 242)

For the dip

4 tablespoons pomegranate
molasses

2 tablespoons walnuts, in pieces

4 tablespoons red pepper paste

Boil the squash in a pan with enough water to cover until
it is soft but not mushy. Drain very well and leave to cool
in the colander.

Blend the onion in a food processor, then, using a sieve,
squeeze as much of the water out as you can. Return to the
food processor.

Add the squash, bulgur, salt, and pepper to the food
processor and blend well. Pour into a large mixing bowl,
add the flour, and knead very well with your hands. Leave
to rest in the fridge for at least 30 minutes.

Meanwhile, make the stuffing by frying the onion in a
bit of oil over low heat until caramelized. Add the spices
and fry for a couple of minutes, stirring to coat, then
add the spinach, walnuts, chickpeas, and molasses. When
the spinach has wilted, take off the heat and let cool.

Take the dough mixture out of the fridge and divide it into
individual balls each slightly smaller than a golf ball. Having
a small bowl of water next to you for dipping your hands
will help to make them smooth. Make sure you knead each
piece really well before rolling into a ball, then use your
forefinger to carve out a hole while rotating the ball with the
other hand. You should end up with a hollow egg-shaped
shell with a thin outer edge. Be careful not to tear the shell.

Put 1 teaspoon of the stuffing inside and seal the ball by
pinching the edge. If the outside breaks slightly once you
have stuffed and sealed it, use a bit of the water to smooth
over the tear. Make each ball into an oval shape with
a little pointy edge on one side using your fingertips.
If you find this difficult, you can just make normal balls.

Deep-fry the balls in vegetable oil for about 5 minutes,
until they turn golden brown. Serve with the dip, which you
make by stirring all the ingredients together in a bowl.

Brunch & Lunch

Breakfast in Syria is all about savory tastes. It's tradition for the family to gather around a smorgasbord of simple delicacies, usually a few olives, homemade labneh drizzled with olive oil, a bunch of fresh mint leaves, tomatoes, cheese, and—this is absolutely essential—tea. The key ingredient, of course, is bread—if you're in a hurry, you make a quick sandwich and munch it on the go; if you've got a little more time, you sit and relax and chat. If you want to step it up a bit, you can fry some eggs with cumin or maybe tomatoes for everyone to dip into with little scoops of bread (almost everything is eaten this way in Syria; the technique has to be perfected at an early age).

Of course, all of this can get a bit grander on the weekend. In Syria we're talking brunch on a Friday rather than Sunday, as that is the main day off work. Friday brunch can be a big social event at home with relatives coming 'round, and the full Syrian breakfast, as it were, is all about ful and fetteh—big, hearty bean and chickpea dishes.

Warm Fava Beans in Olive Oil
(Ful bil Zeit)

In Syrian culture, there's a general rule that men don't do the cooking, with three exceptions: ful, fetteh, and barbecues. There is something rugged about these dishes that reassures even the most traditional kitchen-fearing Arab man enough to feel comfortable in his masculinity preparing them. Ful (fava beans)—whether we're talking the version with olive oil or the one in tahini sauce—is the classic staple of Damascus and Aleppo street food.

What we've been able to work out from the Syrians we've met is that ful must be boiled to perfection in large copper urns, marinated in lemon, garlic, and cumin dressing, then mixed with tomato and parsley. Abu Abdo's, the ful maker's shop in Aleppo, is a landmark that is more than a century old. Abu Abdo himself passed away a long time ago, but generations of his children and grandchildren have passed on the secrets of the trade and kept the business going. Before the war, if you wanted a takeout, Abu Abdo poured the ful into a plastic bag and tied it up, but we won't judge you if you use Tupperware!

Below is a simpler version of the traditional recipe you find in the ful maker's, which we learned from Rana, who makes this at home quite often. Look for cans of "ful mdemmes" in any Middle Eastern supermarket. If you want to cook your fava beans from dried, soak 5 ounces/150 g dried brown fava beans overnight in water to cover, then drain and place in a large pot in enough water to cover. Bring to a boil and cook for about 2 hours on high heat. Keep checking water levels throughout.

SERVES 4 AS PART OF A MEZZE

1 (14-ounce/400 g) can fava beans

2 garlic cloves, crushed

2 tomatoes, diced

Handful of parsley, finely chopped

1 teaspoon ground cumin

Juice of 1 lemon

Salt to taste

Extra-virgin olive oil,
to serve

Pour the beans and their liquid into a pan and heat over medium-low for 10 minutes. Meanwhile, mix the garlic, tomatoes, parsley, cumin, lemon juice, and salt to make the dressing.

Drain the beans, add the dressing, and mix well. Serve drizzled with olive oil.

Chickpeas with Cumin

(Ballila)

Similar to the fava beans, ballila is a traditional dish with one of the longest histories in Syria. It's eaten all over the country, mainly just with bread. It's best served warm.

When we first went to meet Razan (page 194), in Huddersfield, she arrived at her deli with her hands full of equipment—we thought we were just there to chat! But Razan had brought a pan of chickpeas and boxes full of ingredients. As we chatted, she started putting together ballila and told us her next project is to open a little Syrian restaurant, which would serve lots of vegan dishes—"Not because we are catering to vegans, but because many Syrian dishes happen to be vegan." So next time you're in Yorkshire, be sure to look out for Razan's restaurant and this recipe.

SERVES 4 AS PART OF A MEZZE

1(14-ounce/400 g) can chickpeas

1 garlic clove, crushed

Juice of 1 lemon

Generous amount of extra-virgin olive oil

1 tomato, finely diced

Handful of parsley, finely chopped

1 teaspoon ground cumin

Salt and pepper, to taste

Pour the chickpeas and their liquid into a small saucepan. Simmer over low heat for about 10 minutes, until the chickpeas are warmed through.

Make a dressing by whisking together the garlic, lemon juice, and a good pour of olive oil.

Remove from the heat, pour off some of the liquid so it's not like a soup, and add the tomato, parsley, cumin, and salt and pepper and stir. Toss with the dressing.

Fava Beans in Tahini

(Ful bi Tahini)

This variation of the traditional Ful bil Zeit on page 66 is a richer, fuller recipe. You'll find it in any good "ful" restaurant in Syria, the kind that is usually only open until lunchtime. Most Syrians would consider it an aberration to have this as part of a mezze, as it is predominantly a breakfast/brunch dish.

It is best served slightly warm, but be careful not to mix the warm beans with the yogurt too soon, or it will curdle.

SERVES 2 FOR BRUNCH

1 garlic clove

Salt, to taste

4 tablespoons tahini

4 tablespoons plain yogurt

Juice of ½ lemon

1 (14-ounce/400 g) can fava beans

½ tomato, chopped

Handful of parsley, roughly chopped

1 teaspoon ground cumin

Extra-virgin olive oil, for drizzling

Using a pestle and mortar, mix the garlic and salt into a paste.

In a large bowl, mix the garlic paste, tahini, yogurt, and lemon juice and give it a good stir.

Heat the fava beans and their liquid in a saucepan until warmed but not boiling—you don't need to cook them just warm them through. Pour the beans and half of their liquid (discard the rest) into the yogurt mix and stir well. Make sure the beans aren't too hot, or you will curdle the yogurt.

Add the tomato, parsley, and cumin to add color and freshness to the dish.

Eggs with Potatoes and Cumin
(Mufarraket Batata)

When we were traveling around researching this book, one of the things that struck us most was the uncanny ability of the Syrians we met to cook and even play host in the most precarious situations. In Lesbos, we met a group of Syrian youngsters camping in a scrappy public park waiting for registration papers. They had somehow managed to lay their hands on a tiny gas stove that they were using to make Syrian coffee and scramble some eggs with cumin for breakfast.

This dish is bursting with flavor and is so comforting and homey; it's often made for pregnant women, as it is believed to be a reliable detoxifier.

SERVES 2

1 teaspoon butter

1 tablespoon olive oil

2 medium russet potatoes, diced into ½-inch/1 cm cubes

4 garlic cloves, chopped

3 eggs

¼ teaspoon ground cumin

Salt and pepper, to taste

Heat the butter and oil in a frying pan, and fry the potatoes for a few minutes, then add around 4 tablespoons of water and leave to simmer with a lid on—the idea is to steam rather than boil them. Add more water as needed.

When the potatoes have softened, add the garlic and continue to cook with a lid on for a few minutes, then crack the eggs on top and cover. If you prefer scrambled eggs, simply stir the mixture. Season with the cumin, salt, and pepper before serving.

Za'atar Flatbread

(Mana'eesh)

If there's one thing that Syrians can't live without, it's mana'eesh (singular man'ousha). In the same way that pubs are a huge part of life in Britain, mana'eesh bakeries are integral to Syrian culture. Every street corner has one, if not two, of these bakeries. Every morning, no matter where you live, some bakery nearby will be wafting the unmistakable aroma of baked bread, thyme, and melted cheese up to your window, and you'll find yourself unable to resist darting out. Think of a man'ousha as a fragrant Syrian pizza that you can eat for breakfast. What's not to love about that?

The joy of it is the fantastic fresh bread itself. Many bakers will start work as early as 5 a.m. or before, preparing the dough, before applying the different toppings. All of them offer pretty much the same menu: za'atar, cheese, ground meat, labneh, or red pepper paste, but each of these is the baker's own special recipe—and some are definitely better than others. In Syria people tend to be fiercely loyal to their favorite man'ousha bakery.

Being as cheap and readily available as they are, not many people make their own mana'eesh at home, so we have this recipe as an homage to the original. It's a very easy recipe that you can whip up in a jiffy as a starter or light lunch served with salad.

SERVES 6

5 tablespoons extra-virgin olive oil

3 tablespoons za'atar

1 (14-ounce/400 g) frozen puff pastry, defrosted overnight in the refrigerator

½ tomato, diced, to serve

Fresh mint leaves, to serve

Preheat the oven to 320°F/160°C. Line a baking sheet with parchment. Mix the olive oil with the za'atar.

Unfold the pastry on the prepared baking sheet and, using a pastry brush, spread the za'atar olive oil all over, leaving a 1-inch/2.5 cm border around the edges.

Bake in the oven for about 15 minutes, until the pastry puffs up and turns golden brown.

Serve with tomato and fresh mint on top.

Stuffed Pastries

(Fatayer)

Every bakery in Syria will serve fatayer, triangle pies filled with lemony spinach, cheese, or labneh. They are a favorite breakfast or brunch snack for many.

In Beirut, we visited Zarifa's home in the Shatila camp. With a tiny kitchen that only had space for a sink, she cooked everything on a camping gas stove in her narrow hallway. Such proud hosts are the Syrians that this didn't deter her from serving us an absolute feast. We asked how she made the fatayer without an oven, and she replied, "I made the dough and the stuffing here and took it to the baker, who made the fatayer and baked them in his oven."

For the dough

2⅓ cups/300 g all-purpose flour

½ teaspoon instant yeast

½ teaspoon granulated sugar

½ teaspoon salt

⅔ cup/150 ml warm milk
(plus more if needed)

3 tablespoons/45 ml vegetable oil

1 egg, lightly beaten, for brushing

For the cheese stuffing

5 ounces/130 g halloumi, grated

5 ounces/130 g mozzarella, grated

1½ cups/80 g parsley leaves,
finely chopped

1 tablespoon nigella seeds

For the labneh stuffing

12 cherry tomatoes, finely diced

6 small labneh balls, broken,
or 4 tablespoons spreadable
labneh (page 56)

2 small Persian cucumbers,
finely diced

Small handful of fresh mint,
finely chopped

2 tablespoons olive oil

Salt, to taste

For the spinach stuffing

1 onion, finely chopped

Olive oil, for frying

10 ounces/300 g spinach, chopped

4 teaspoons sumac

Juice of 1 lemon

A handful of pomegranate seeds

Salt and pepper, to taste

Mix all the dry ingredients for the dough in a bowl. Add the milk and the oil bit by bit until the mixture forms a pliable dough, then knead it very well. Transfer to an oiled bowl in a warm place until it doubles in size (around an hour, but the longer the better). Note: to make all three stuffing options, triple the dough.

Preheat the oven to 350°F/180°C.

Meanwhile, make the stuffing of your choice. If you're making cheese or labneh, simply mix the ingredients together.

If you're making the spinach stuffing, over very low heat, fry the onion in a little olive oil for 20 to 30 minutes, until softened and almost caramelized. Add the spinach leaves and cook them until wilted, then sprinkle on the sumac, lemon juice, pomegranate seeds, and salt and pepper, and stir. Leave to cool.

Roll the dough out so that it is about ⅛ inch/3 mm thick and, using a 3.5-inch/9 cm glass or cutter, cut out circles. We use a dumpling mold to create a perfect shape: place the circle of dough on the mold, fill it with 1 generous teaspoon whichever stuffing you are using, then close and seal. If you don't have a mold, you can do it by hand just as easily by folding the circle over and sealing with your fingertips. Repeat until all the stuffing and dough is used up.

Once you have finished all the dough, place the fatayer on a baking sheet, brush with beaten egg, and bake for 10 to 13 minutes, until golden.

Eggs with Tomatoes and Cumin
(Shuzmuz)

Shuzmuz is the Syrian answer to shakshuka or Turkish menemen. In Arabic, if something is really tasty we say, "Watch out, or you'll eat your fingers with it." Itab's dad would say that to her every time she cooked this for him.

In Syria you traditionally eat it on a Friday morning with flatbread and fresh raw green peppers for a crunch and an extra hit of vitamin C. Even on the wettest, windiest day in western Europe, this is a dish that makes us feel like we are sitting on the balcony of a house in the Mediterranean, watching the sun come up.

SERVES 2

1 small onion

1 teaspoon butter

½ green bell pepper

2 medium tomatoes, diced

4 eggs, beaten

Salt and pepper, to taste

Ground cumin to taste

Ground Aleppo pepper, to taste (optional)

Fry the onion in the butter in a frying pan over medium heat until it is soft. Add the green pepper and continue to fry for about 5 more minutes, then add the tomatoes and fry until everything is soft and slightly mushy.

Add salt and pepper to the eggs, then pour into the frying pan and stir, as you would for scrambled eggs. Keep stirring so that the egg doesn't stick to the pan.

Add the cumin and Aleppo pepper, if using, and serve immediately with warm bread.

Syrian Omelette
(Ijja)

Before the conflict began, there was a little restaurant in a hidden corner of a back alley in Aleppo's Old City, next to the old Jewish cemetery. The restaurant was called the King of Omelettes (Malik Al Ijja) and aptly named it was, too. The place was so tiny, they could only cram in two customers at a time, and there was only one thing on the menu: Aleppian omelettes. People from all around the ancient souq flocked to it every lunchtime and lined up to get a taste. Celebrities from all over Syria came to visit, and the owner proudly covered his front window with pictures of himself and the famous people. The place was shabby and unpretentious, and it operated for generations without ever changing a thing. We're not sure whether this restaurant is still there. We loved it, and now we're passing on its secret.

MAKES 7 SMALL OMELETTES

6 large eggs

1 onion, grated

1 medium zucchini, grated (optional)

Big bunch of parsley, finely chopped

2 tablespoons all-purpose flour

Salt and pepper, to taste

½ teaspoon ground Aleppo pepper

½ teaspoon ground cumin

Vegetable oil, for frying

In a mixing bowl, add the eggs, onion, zucchini, if using, and parsley and mix well. Stir in the flour and add the salt, pepper, and spices. It should make a nice thick batter.

Heat 3 tablespoons of oil in a frying pan over medium heat. Scoop one small ladle of the batter and pour it into the middle of the pan. Level it out a little with a spatula so that it is about ½ inch/1 cm thick, but no more. Cook for 2 minutes, then flip onto the other side and cook for a further 1 to 2 minutes. Each side should be light brown in color. Repeat with the remaining batter, adding more oil as needed.

Traditionally this is served with Ayran (see page 224), or just plain yogurt. It tastes great with a squeeze of lemon juice, too.

Falafel Wrap

Falafel, like hummus, is perhaps one of the few Syrian staples that needs no introduction. It has made its way into the hearts and stomachs of Western food lovers and is there to stay. You can buy ready-made falafel in almost any corner shop these days, but if you have ever tried fresh falafel in the Middle East, you'll never dream of buying it again.

Falafel originated in Egypt as "ta'miyeh," where they make it with fava beans, but in Syria—and the rest of the Arab world—it is made with chickpeas, or a mixture of the two.

On our trips to Lebanon and Syria, the first thing we craved when we touched down in Beirut was a steaming, crispy, unctuous falafel wrap. Not many people make it at home, so we went to a tiny local falafel stall and spent the morning with their staff learning how to make it. It caused quite a stir among their customers, who all crowded around to see why there were two women behind the counters making and serving falafel. Dina received at least one marriage proposal.

You can buy a special device online if you want to shape them the traditional way, but to be honest, we've found you can make the balls with your hands just as well—they taste the same. Another idea is to stuff your falafel with chile sauce if you want to give them a bit of a kick. To do that you just need to make the balls slightly bigger, and with your finger make a little hole in the middle for the chile, then seal it up, dip in sesame seeds (to differentiate them from the non-chile-filled ones), and deep-fry as normal.

SERVES 4–6

1 medium onion, peeled and quartered

1½ cups/250 g dried chickpeas, soaked overnight in hot water

2 garlic cloves, crushed

Large bunch of parsley, chopped

Large bunch of cilantro, chopped

1 teaspoon salt

½ teaspoon baking soda

½ teaspoon ground cumin

½ teaspoon ground coriander

Sesame seeds (optional), for coating

Approximately 2 cups/500 ml vegetable oil, for deep-frying

For a falafel wrap (optional)

Flatbread

Chopped tomatoes

Chopped Pickled Turnips (page 234)

Pickled Cucumbers, sliced (page 239)

Tahini Sauce (page 243)

A few leaves of fresh mint and fresh parsley

Blend the onion in the food processor, then put to one side.

Next, blend the chickpeas, garlic, parsley, and cilantro very well and pour the mixture into a bowl. Add the onion, salt, baking soda, cumin, and coriander and mix well using your hands. Divide the mixture into little balls and, if you want, roll them in some sesame seeds. If the mixture is too wet and doesn't stick together, add a little all-purpose flour.

Pour the oil in a pan so it is at least 2 inches/5 cm deep and heat. When the oil is very hot, gently lower the falafel into the oil using a metal spoon and cook in batches until they become crisp and dark on the outside, but still green on the inside, 5 to 10 minutes.

Place a paper towel on a plate and, using a slotted spoon, take the cooked falafel out of the oil and put on the plate to soak up any excess oil.

To make an authentic Syrian falafel sandwich, roughly squash three falafel balls onto a flatbread. Add chopped tomatoes, chopped turnip pickles, cucumber pickles, Tahini Sauce, and a few leaves of fresh mint and fresh parsley, then roll into a wrap and eat immediately.

Hala

We met Hala in Damascus in 2010 while we were working on a theater project there. She is an artist and poet who worked as a lecturer at the University of Damascus, then moved to the U.K. for her master's degree in graphic design, followed by a PhD on the conflict in Syria.

Hala has always loved food, but when she lived in Damascus cooking was never of any interest to her; she was too engrossed in painting, writing poems, her career, and her social life. It was only in the last three or four years while living with her English husband in Kent and writing a dissertation that she developed a passion for cooking. Four thousand kilometers from home, it was a choice between English food or learning to cook the food that she yearned for from home. It wasn't a difficult decision.

In Aleppo, where she grew up, Hala's mother was known as the Queen of Kibbeh—and it was through choppy Skype conversations or WhatsApp voice messages that Hala learned to cook her mother's special recipes.

On Christmas Eve in 2015 she cooked a Syrian meal of Mtabak (page 52), Maqloubeh (page 130), and Tabbouleh (page 60) for her in-laws from Macclesfield, followed by a British Christmas lunch. "My mother-in-law couldn't believe how many eggplants I used," she told us.

It's too dangerous for Hala to visit Syria very often, but on the few occasions she can make it through, she always returns with parcels of her mother's food vacuum-packed, so that she can take as much as possible. She also brings over za'atar, baby zucchini, and eggplant dried in the sun until they're thin and flat. Back in Kent, Hala boils them to bring them back to life and produces the most gorgeous sheikh mahshi (stuffed zucchini).

Those visits to Damascus are always strange for Hala. "When I first went back to Damascus I didn't really have an appetite," she said. "The emotional experience took over at first, but eventually I couldn't resist and fatayer were the first things I ate."

Halloumi Wrap

In April 2013, while Hala (see page 86) was in England working on her PhD, her dad, Morris Georges, was tragically killed by a missile while at an ATM one morning. We met Morris with Hala back in 2010 in Damascus' Old City; he was a warm, smiley man who was always making jokes. In that one moment Hala's world was turned upside down, and she has been coming to terms with her loss ever since. Her art and poetry have been hugely influenced by the event, as have her studies—unsurprisingly.

Hala wanted to share this recipe, which her dad always used to make for his three daughters and eight grandchildren. "For me, this is a simple but sacred flavor, as it reminds me of my dad and family times back in Damascus," she told us. She has tried to replicate his recipe here in England, but no matter what method she uses "it's never the same." Maybe the ingredients taste different here, or maybe she doesn't have the right equipment, but we still think it's delicious. He would use a big heavy grill, a bit like the ones you see in cafés that heat up panini. We experimented with a griddle pan and won Hala's approval: "not as good as my dad's but the next best thing."

So, this one's for you, Morris Georges, in loving memory.

MAKES 2 WRAPS

2 Arabic flatbreads

Extra-virgin olive oil, for coating

4 to 8 slices halloumi cheese, lightly grilled on both sides

Dried and fresh mint, to taste

Using a pastry brush, thoroughly coat the bread with olive oil so that it is really covered. Place the halloumi in the middle of the bread and sprinkle it with the dried and fresh mint. Fold the bread over into a wrap and place it on a hot griddle pan. Put something heavy on top and leave for 5 minutes, then turn and repeat.

Labneh Wrap

It is unthinkable to live without labneh in Syria. Go there and you won't find a house without labneh lurking somewhere in the fridge. It is one of the inviolable sacraments of Syrian eating; no one is allowed to say "I don't like it"—it just doesn't happen. When we were cooking with Rana, a 27-year-old mother from Dara'a, she told us that each year she would buy 150 kilos of fresh milk and spend the week turning the milk into food the family could eat year-round. Her recipes would include cheese, kishk (fermented yogurt), and butter, but the labneh was the star. It's a kind of thickened yogurt, the texture of cream cheese, which you can treat as a dip, with olives for breakfast, or in a sandwich. Almost every kid in Syria goes to school with a labneh wrap in their lunch box every morning.

Make sure you eat it with a sweetened cup of tea for the real authentic taste!

MAKES 2 WRAPS

4 to 8 balls/3 tablespoons labneh
(page 56)

2 flatbreads or tortillas

1 tomato, sliced

1 Persian cucumber, julienned

½ green bell pepper, julienned

Fresh mint leaves

Small handful of pitted olives

Extra-virgin olive oil, for drizzling

Salt and pepper, to taste

For each wrap, spread half of the labneh on the bread, then evenly top with the rest of the ingredients, drizzle with olive oil, season with salt and pepper, and fold the bread over into a wrap.

Shawarma Wrap

You might think you know shawarma from your local kebab shop, but you haven't tried it for real until you've been to Syria. Our favorite place to buy shawarma was a tiny booth on the corner of an ancient Roman alleyway in the Old City of Damascus. It's street food that is a million miles from the flaccid efforts you'll find outside the country, with a combination of textures and flavors that has been perfected over decades, if not centuries. The key is really good chicken marinated for hours, then rotated on the grill, crispy on the outside and luscious on the inside. Then there's the creamy, pungent ooze of garlic sauce set against powerful sweet-and-sour pomegranate molasses (not chile sauce!) and tart crispy pickles, all accessed via warm toasted flatbread, which cracks as you bite into it. Here's our best approximation of how to do it.

You can use tortilla wraps rather than flatbread if you want a simpler, quicker option.

For the shawarma

3 tablespoons vegetable oil, plus more for frying

1 tablespoon plain yogurt

1 teaspoon freshly ground cardamom

½ teaspoon ground coriander

Salt and pepper, to taste

2 boneless, skinless chicken breasts, very thinly sliced

For the wrap

Garlic Sauce (see below)

6 flatbreads

2 pickled cucumbers (page 239) or 6 gherkins

Pomegranate molasses, for drizzling

First, prepare the shawarma. Mix the oil, yogurt, cardamom, coriander, and salt and pepper. Add the chicken and marinate in the yogurt sauce for at least 30 minutes or up to 8 hours.

Remove the chicken slices from the marinade and shallow-fry them in oil in a pan over medium heat until slightly browned.

Spread the garlic sauce onto the flatbreads, then top with some of the chicken strips and pickled cucumbers and drizzle with pomegranate molasses.

Roll up the bread around the ingredients and place it in a frying pan held down with a weighted lid for a couple of minutes—a pestle and mortar works great, or a heavy pan. Turn and repeat on the other side. Repeat for the 5 remaining flatbreads.

Garlic Sauce

(Sos El Toum)

This is a dairy- and gluten-free, eggless sauce. Shawarma places around the country use large amounts of it because it lasts longer, is less fatty, and is much cheaper to make than garlic mayonnaise.

MAKES 1½ CUPS

2 tablespoons cornstarch

2 garlic cloves, crushed

2 tablespoons lemon juice

2 tablespoons vegetable oil

Salt, to taste

Dissolve the cornstarch in a bit of cold water. Heat 1¼ cups/ 300 ml of water in a pan, then add the dissolved cornstarch. Stir quickly with a whisk. Remove the pan from the heat once the liquid reaches a thick consistency. Transfer to a bowl and place in the fridge to cool.

Meanwhile, mix together the garlic, lemon, oil, and salt. Add the cornstarch mix once it has cooled down and blend everything in a food processor until smooth. Store in the fridge for up to 2 weeks.

Roasted Cauliflower Wrap

While researching this book in Beirut, one of our favorite late-night snacks was a cauliflower wrap from Abu Toni's take-away at the end of our street. On our way home, or when we took a much-needed break, we would treat ourselves to one of these and devour the flavors. We sometimes went back for a second wrap, because we just couldn't get enough of it.

MAKES 2 WRAPS

1 cauliflower, cut into florets

Vegetable oil, for roasting

Salt and pepper, to taste

2 flatbreads

4 pieces of Pickled Turnip (page 234)

4 pieces of Pickled Cucumber (page 239)

1 tomato, sliced

Small handful of parsley leaves

Tahini Sauce (page 243), for drizzling

Preheat the oven to 350°F/180°C.

Roast the cauliflower florets with some oil and salt and pepper for about 30 minutes, until they start to turn dark brown in color.

Place some of the roasted cauliflower florets in the middle of each piece of bread, then add the pickles, tomato, parsley, and a generous helping of the Tahini Sauce.

Roll the breads into wraps and devour immediately.

Freekeh Soup

(Shorbet Freekeh)

Six years ago, when Itab first moved to London, she invited her future British in-laws for dinner. She slow-cooked a leg of lamb with Syrian spices and served it on a bed of freekeh. No one had heard of freekeh back then, and her mother-in-law, Lindsay, who is an excellent cook, was fascinated by this exotic, smoky-green wheat. She started making it for her friends, who were equally impressed. Itab is convinced that she's the sole reason why freekeh is now the trendy grain on London's most fashionable dining tables!

SERVES 4

1 pound/500 g cubed lamb, from the leg or shoulder

Vegetable oil, for frying

2 bay leaves

1 medium-sized cinnamon stick

5 cloves

5 cardamom pods

1½ cups/250 g freekeh, rinsed well

1 tablespoon salt

1 onion, chopped

1 carrot, peeled and chopped

1 tablespoon tomato paste (optional)

4 ounces/100 g frozen peas (optional)

Fry the lamb in a hot saucepan or casserole with a lid in a bit of oil for a couple of minutes until browned all over. Add 6 cups of water so that it just covers the meat, bring to a boil, then turn the heat down to a simmer, skimming off any bits that collect on the surface as you go along. After about 15 minutes, add the bay leaves and cinnamon stick to the lamb. Put the cloves and cardamom in a spice bag or knotted piece of cheesecloth and add that too.

Add the freekeh to the lamb, along with the salt, onion, and carrot and simmer with the lid on for about 45 minutes to 1 hour. You will need to add as much as 2 cups of additional water, as the freekah cooks.

If you want to go for a tomato flavor, squeeze in some tomato paste halfway through the cooking time. Leave to simmer and then add the peas, if using, in the last 10 minutes. Remove the spice bag and serve piping hot.

Vegan Freekeh Soup
(Shorbet Freekeh Nabatiyeh)

The sweetness of the peas and carrots in this vegan version really complements the smokiness of the freekeh. It's a very simple recipe, yet substantial enough to have for lunch with a bit of bread or a salad on the side.

SERVES 4

Vegetable oil, for frying

1 onion, chopped

1 medium-sized cinnamon stick

1 bay leaf

½ teaspoon black peppercorns

2 carrots, peeled and diced

1½ cups/250 g freekeh, rinsed well

4 cups/1 L vegetable stock
(page 247)

4 ounces/100 g frozen peas

Heat some oil in a large pan over medium heat, then add the onion, cinnamon stick, bay leaf, and peppercorns and fry for a few minutes until the onion has softened. Add the carrots and continue to fry for a couple of minutes before adding the freekeh.

Pour in the stock and bring to a boil, then reduce the heat, add the peas, and simmer for about 30 minutes with the lid on. You may need to add as much as 1 cup/250 ml of additional stock or water, depending on how thick you like your soup. Serve piping hot.

Red Lentil Soup
(Shorbet Addas)

If you are eating out for Iftar during Ramadan, any restaurant will give you this soup without you having to order it, as it is an absolutely essential step in breaking your fast. However, it's not exclusive to Ramadan at all; in fact, it's a year-round staple—filling, addictive, and good for the tummy.

When we were visiting women in refugee camps in the Beka'a Valley in Lebanon, one of the women took us to a newly opened Syrian restaurant where we had the most delicious version of this soup. Ultimate comfort food.

SERVES 4

1¾ cups/300 g dry split red lentils

1 teaspoon butter

1 onion, diced

4 garlic gloves, crushed

½ teaspoon ground turmeric

½ teaspoon ground cumin

5 cups/1.2 L vegetable stock (page 247)

1 flatbread

Olive oil, for brushing

Juice of 1 lemon

Salt and pepper, to taste

1 onion, sliced (optional), to serve

Sliced radishes to serve

Lemon, cut in wedges

Rinse the lentils a couple of times in a sieve and drain. Heat the butter in a pan, add 1 diced onion, and fry for a few minutes, then add the garlic and fry for one more minute. Add the lentils, turmeric, and cumin, followed by the stock and bring to a boil.

Turn the heat down and simmer with a lid on for 20 minutes, stirring regularly so that the lentils don't stick to the bottom of the pan. If it gets too thick, just add some water.

Preheat the oven to 350°F/180°C. Brush the flatbread with olive oil all over, cut into squares, and place in the oven for 5 minutes until crispy and brown.

When the lentils are completely soft, turn off the heat and carefully purée well with a blender. Pour the soup back into the pan, squeeze in the lemon juice, and season with salt and pepper. Serve with sliced onion (if using), sliced radishes, crispy flatbread, and wedges of lemon.

Lentil and Chard Soup

(Shorbet Addas wa Silig)

This is definitely one of those dishes that takes us back in time to sitting around a gas heater on a cold Damascene day, the fire crackling, heads bent as we hungrily sipped away on this soup. Not only is it healthy, fresh, and flavorful, it's also very very addictive—so watch out! For those with big appetites like ours, these quantities serve two people, but if you're a more modest eater, it should be enough for four.

SERVES 2–4

Vegetable oil, for frying
1 medium onion, peeled and sliced
3 garlic cloves, crushed
4 cups/1 L vegetable stock
½ cup/100 g brown lentils
1 medium potato, peeled and cubed
8 ounces/225 g chard, chopped
Handful of cilantro leaves
½ teaspoon ground cumin
Salt and pepper, to taste
Juice of 1 lemon
Extra-virgin olive oil, for drizzling

Heat the oil in a frying pan and, over low heat, slowly fry the onion until caramelized—it should take about 30 minutes or so. Add the garlic about halfway through the cooking time.

In a separate pan, bring the stock and lentils to a boil, then turn the heat down and simmer, covered, for 20 minutes.

Add the potatoes to the lentils and continue to simmer for a further 5 minutes before adding the chard.

When the lentils and potatoes are tender, stir in the cilantro, cumin, caramelized onions and garlic, and some salt, pepper, and lemon juice. Drizzle with olive oil and serve immediately.

Tahani

Tahani gave birth to her son, Ahmed, under siege. When news got out, a neighbor appeared at her door, begging her to breastfeed her own newborn girl. By then, in Douma, anything edible had become a priceless luxury, and the mother was so malnourished (or perhaps traumatized) that she couldn't produce any milk. Bottled milk was rarer and more expensive than gold. Tahani thought of her own fragile health and her own baby, but the child in front of her was so desperately skinny, she couldn't find it in herself to say no. Miraculously, all three pulled through. It was God Almighty, she is sure, who helped her get two babies through months of starvation. Throughout Syria, in areas under siege, new mothers can be found looking for others who could breastfeed. Not everyone is so lucky.

We met Tahani in a rented house in an obscure village near the Jordanian border. Thirty-six months under siege had brought her very close to starvation, but somehow she had managed to get out to Damascus and smuggle herself and her baby onto a bus heading south, where her mother awaited her with bowls of her favorite mloukhia (jute leaf stew) and okra stew.

"I dove into them and ate like a wolf," she told us. "I ate so much my tummy hurt badly for a few days after, as it wasn't used to nutritious, rich food—but who cares, it was all worth it."

Jute Leaf Soup
(Shorbet Mloukhia)

Mloukhia can be traced back to ancient Egypt, and legend has it that the name comes from the Arabic word for "king," *melik*, so it means "the dish of the kings."

Mloukhia occupies a huge space in Egyptian cuisine, but Syrians love it just as much. We ran a workshop with a group of Syrian women living in Beirut, and when we asked them what they would cook if they had English guests over for dinner, mloukhia was on all of their lists. It's not the easiest ingredient to find in the West; in English, according to the dictionary, *mloukhia* goes by the name "jute leaves." We found dried ones on Edgware Road in London, which has been dominated by Arab shops and restaurants for decades now and is well stocked with some of our key ingredients. So look online, or seek out your local Arab shop and they'll no doubt have some.

SERVES 2

0.35 ounce/10 g dried jute leaves
1 garlic clove, crushed
½ teaspoon ground coriander
Olive oil, for frying
1 vegetable stock cube
¼ teaspoon salt
Juice of ½ lemon

Grind the leaves by rubbing them together with your fingers until they are very fine. Remove any woody stalks.

Fry the garlic and corinader in a little bit of olive oil, add the ground jute leaves, then pour in 2 cups/500 ml of water and bring to a boil. Add the stock cube and salt, then simmer for about 10 minutes.

Take off the heat, add the lemon juice, then serve.

Main Courses

It's hard to believe that after a table full of mezze you would have room for more, but when you visit the home of a Syrian, you need to bring an appetite. Mezze is big and they're not really "starters," so larger dishes are likely to arrive while there is still a plethora of small plates on the table, turning a meal into a feast as you work your way through pickles, yogurt, and salad even before the main courses. While many mezze dishes are vegetarian, most main courses feature lamb, beef, or chicken. But even now, vegetables still play the most important role, so much so that a dish will almost always be named for its central vegetable, with the meat taking the supporting role—for example, Green Bean and Lamb Stew, or White Bean and Lamb Stew. Historically this may be due to the relative scarcity and costliness of meat, but the results are far more interesting, in our opinion.

The Wandering Jew or The Fleeing Muslim

(Yahoudi Msafer/ Muslim Harban)

Perhaps not the most politically correct dish on Earth, but there's little better to tuck into on a hot Damascene summer day. One story goes that the dish originated with the Jews of Damascus, supposedly because the Jews of the city used to cook it for people who were traveling. Oddly enough the Jews themselves call it "the fleeing Muslim." As you'd expect in this region, this is all very controversial—and it's not just the name, but also how you cook it. The only thing people agree on is that the main ingredient is bulgur wheat. Some people cook it with zucchini, others with eggplant, and some add tomatoes to the bulgur. We thought it best to avoid the controversy and just give you all the options.

It makes a great addition to a barbecue or summer picnic, as it tastes just as good served cold.

SERVES 4

1 teaspoon butter

1 onion, diced

5 large ripe tomatoes, grated or blended in a food processor, or 1(14-ounce/400 g) can chopped tomatoes, plus extra diced tomatoes to serve on the side

½ teaspoon salt

Black pepper, to taste

1¼ cups/200 g coarse bulgur wheat, rinsed a couple of times and drained

¾ cup/200 ml vegetable stock

Extra-virgin olive oil, to serve

Eggplant or zucchini, fried or roasted (optional)

Melt the butter in a saucepan and fry the onion for about 5 minutes until soft.

Add the tomatoes, salt, and pepper and simmer with a lid on for 30 minutes, stirring occasionally.

Next, add the drained bulgur and the stock and simmer over the lowest heat for 10 to 15 minutes. Test the bulgur to make sure it's tender; if not, cook it a little longer.

Pour onto a large plate or into a bowl, drizzle with a generous amount of extra-virgin olive oil, and serve with fresh tomatoes or your chosen vegetable.

Stuffed Eggplant

(Fetteh Makdous)

Fetteh Makdous is a dish from Damascus that uses pretty much everything that is quintessentially Syrian and is very similar to its vegetarian sister, Fetteh Beitinjaan (Eggplant Fetteh), with the addition of meat and tomato sauce.

SERVES 4

2 medium eggplants

Vegetable oil, for frying

6 ounces/150 g ground beef

1 generous tablespoon butter

3 large tomatoes, halved and grated to remove the skin

1½ tablespoons tomato paste

½ cup/8 tablespoons Tahini Sauce (page 243)

3 tablespoons toasted pine nuts

Handful of parsley, finely chopped

2 flatbreads, toasted and broken into little pieces

Peel the eggplants lengthwise in strips 1 to 2 cm apart until you are left with the stripy effect all the way around. Slice thinly lengthwise. Fry in a pan, or roast them in the oven at 350°F/180°C for 40 minutes, in a generous amount of oil. Set aside on top of a few layers of paper towel to drain off some of the oil.

Meanwhile, fry the meat in a frying pan with a little oil over low heat until brown and soft.

Next, melt the butter in a separate frying pan, add the tomatoes and tomato paste and simmer for 20 to 30 minutes, or until thickened. Stir occasionally.

To assemble, pour the tomato sauce in a flat dish. Put 1 teaspoon of the meat on one slice of eggplant, then roll. Repeat until you finish all the eggplant slices and place them in the tomato sauce. Spoon over the Tahini Sauce.

Top with toasted pine nuts and chopped parsley and whatever meat mixture is left over. Serve with toasted bread.

Brown Lentils and Bulgur

(Mjadara)

An ancient recipe, mjadara is an age-old source of low-cost flavor and calories, but today it is eaten by rich and poor alike. However, it's still that sense of humility that makes it a particularly popular dish for Christians during Lent. When we were kids, in order to encourage us to eat it, our parents would tell us that all the old people survived this long because they had eaten a lot of mjadara.

In many countries this dish is cooked with rice, but in Syria they use coarse bulgur wheat. If you don't eat wheat, you can replace the bulgur with basmati rice.

It's perfect comfort food that you can make when you don't have any food in the house, and it's equally yummy eaten hot or at room temperature; a bit of plain yogurt on the side and a tomato and cucumber salad is all you need. Don't worry if the lentils turn a bit mushy; that's the idea.

SERVES 4

1 cup/200 g dried brown lentils, rinsed a couple of times and drained

⅓ cup/80 ml vegetable oil

2 to 3 large onions, sliced

1 cup/200 g coarse bulgur wheat, rinsed a couple of times and drained

1 teaspoon salt

1 teaspoon 7 spices (page 244)

Extra-virgin olive oil, for drizzling

Add the lentils to a pan and cover with 3 cups/700 ml of water. Bring to a boil over medium heat then reduce to a simmer and let the lentils cook for about 15 minutes with the lid on.

Heat the oil in a frying pan over medium heat and fry the onions until softened. Remove half of the onions and set aside. Fry the remaining onions until they are brown and crispy, then remove from the heat.

Add the softened onions, bulgur, salt, and 7 spices to the lentils, stir once, and simmer over low heat with the lid on until the water has evaporated and the mjadara is tender, without a bite.

Serve with the crispy onions on top and a generous drizzle of extra-virgin olive oil.

Burnt Fingers

(Huraag Usba'u)

People in Damascus are famous all over Syria for the bizarre but evocative names they give their dishes, and Burnt Fingers is no exception. It is meant to be eaten cold, but legend has it that no one could wait for this delicious dish to cool down and would burn their fingers when tucking in. That smell of caramelized onions and the sweet-and-sour taste of tamarind instantly transports Syrians back to the alleys of the Old City of Damascus and the period dramas everyone watched during Ramadan as kids. The preparation of the dish is a big Ramadan tradition, and all the women of the family would get together in the morning to roll out the dough.

It's a great excuse to get creative with the presentation—making patterns out of the golden croutons, the lush cilantro, and the deep brown lentils and onions. And don't worry about making too much—it will only taste better the next day.

We love making the crispy croutons for this as they're so simple and delicious, but if you don't have time, you could use toasted flatbread instead. When we made these with Mona (see page 128), she didn't have a pastry cutter and improvised with her wedding ring, which we thought was rather apt, given the name of the dish.

SERVES 6

For the croutons (you could use toasted flatbread instead)

½ cup/70 g all-purpose flour

Pinch of salt

For the lentils

1⅓ cups/250 g dried brown lentils, rinsed well

1 zucchini, diced

2 garlic cloves, crushed

1½ tablespoons tamarind paste

1 generous tablespoon pomegranate molasses

Vegetable oil, for deep-frying

2 onions, sliced

½ teaspoon salt

Bunch of cilantro, roughly chopped

First make the dough for the croutons. Combine the flour and salt and gradually add in water as you go along, a little at a time, starting with a few tablespoons, until there is no dry flour. Knead into a dough for about 10 minutes, then put in a bowl, cover with a kitchen towel, and leave to rest for 15 minutes.

Put the lentils in a pan, cover with 3½ cups/800 ml of water, and bring to a boil, then lower the heat and simmer, stirring occasionally, for about 20 minutes.

Roll out the dough on a floured surface so it's about ⅛ inch/3 mm thick and cut out little circles (if you don't want to use a ring, you could make squares with a pizza slicer). Make sure they are well floured so they don't stick together.

Once the lentils have been simmering for about 20 minutes, add the zucchini, garlic, tamarind paste, and pomegranate molasses and continue to simmer.

Meanwhile, in a wok or a deep frying pan, heat about 2 inches/5 cm of oil until it is very hot. Fry the onions until they are crisp and brown, but not burnt. Pour half of them into the lentil mixture with a bit of the oil and set the rest to one side.

Add more oil to the pan and deep-fry the dough circles until golden. Remove from the oil with a slotted spoon and set aside on paper towels.

Add the salt and a small handful of cilantro to the lentils, keeping the rest for topping. Once the lentils are soft, pour the contents of the pan into a large bowl, top with the reserved cilantro, fried onions, and croutons.

This can be served hot or cold, just don't burn your fingers!

Green Bean and Tomato Stew with Rice

(Lubiyeh wa Banadoura)

Good-quality ingredients make all the difference with this recipe, and you need little more than a few sweet ripe tomatoes and crunchy runner beans. It's so simple, cheap, and healthy. We love it with plain basmati rice, which turns it into a proper substantial supper, but you can easily serve it as a mezze and scoop it up with some flatbread. Some people make it with beef, which we've included instructions for below.

SERVES 2

Oil, for frying

1 medium onion, diced

4 garlic cloves, peeled and halved

1 pound/450 g green beans, trimmed

6 large ripe tomatoes, cored and blended

2 tablespoons tomato paste

Salt and pepper, to taste

Extra-virgin olive oil, to serve

Hot basmati rice, for serving

Heat the oil in a deep frying pan and fry the onion for 5 to 10 minutes until softened. Add the garlic and beans and fry for 5 more minutes before adding the blended tomatoes.

Bring the sauce to a boil, then simmer for 10 minutes with a lid on. Add the tomato paste, salt, and pepper and continue to simmer for another 20 to 30 minutes, stirring occasionally. If the sauce gets a little dry, add a bit of water.

Once cooked, pour a generous amount of extra-virgin olive oil on top and serve with rice.

Alternative:
You can also make this with beef. Just add 8 ounces/250 g ground beef to the onion and brown the meat before adding the garlic, beans, and tomatoes.

Ahlam

In Beirut we met 36-year-old Ahlam, who loves all things sporty and used to do karate back in Syria. She's a really feisty character and exceptionally good at keepy-uppies (juggling a soccer ball). She told us a wonderful story about a lucky escape—for her, and for her favorite chicken recipe. If ever there was a tale that exemplifies the Syrian love of food and their spirit of defiance, this is it.

When the fighting broke out in Damascus, Ahlam had just bought a chicken to make her special broth for her brother-in-law, who was feeling unwell. As the attacks got closer to their neighborhood, she and her family were forced to suddenly retreat to her uncle's house, where they would be safe from the shelling. She realized then that the chicken had been left at her house.

"I thought, right, there's a chicken in that house, let's go get it." Her husband was too afraid to leave, but in the end she made him drive her there. When they arrived, she said to him, "Give me the key, I'll go." "Do you want to die?!" he replied. "Die or not die, there are children and a family who need feeding," she retorted.

A rocket exploded and her husband dove under the car. Ahlam shouted, "You idiot, give me the keys, quick!" She ran and ran as the mortar shells were falling, until she reached their building, where she bumped into her neighbor, who asked, "What the hell are you doing here?" She was too embarrassed to say she had come to get a chicken. "He'll say this woman is mad!" So she pretended she was getting some "important things."

Ahlam found the chicken in the fridge, still in its pan. She grabbed it and ran back to the car, hiding in people's front porches whenever there was another explosion. "As I was running, I thought, if anything happens to me they'll say, 'Ahlam died for that chicken.' And that's how they'll remember me."

Back in the car she said to her husband, "Hurry up, if a rocket hits us this boiled chicken is going to be a roast chicken!"

They arrived back safely, cooked some freekeh to go with the chicken, and fed four families with it.

Freekeh with Chicken
(Freekeh ma' Jaaj)

Freekeh can come whole or cracked and can be green or yellow-brown in color, depending on how well it has been roasted. You may need to add more stock and cook for longer depending on which type of freekeh you are using. This recipe is for the whole, well-roasted kind. The spices Ahlam (page 120) uses really complement the smoky flavor of freekeh.

You can eat this hot, as we've suggested here, or serve it cold as a salad. Just shred the chicken and, when the freekeh cools down, mix all the ingredients together in a large bowl. This recipe also works beautifully with a leg of lamb coated in the same spices and slow-roasted in the oven.

Vegetable oil, as needed
for chicken

7 cloves

5 cardamom pods

1 cinnamon stick, broken in half

1 (4-pound/2 kg) chicken, cut up

Salt, to taste

Handful of cashews and almonds

Butter, for frying

2 cups/400 g freekeh, rinsed
and drained

Pomegranate seeds (optional)

Olive oil, for drizzling

In a large saucepan, fry the cloves, cardamom, and cinnamon in vegetable oil for a couple of minutes, then add the chicken and fry in batches for a couple more minutes to coat in the spices.

Cover the chicken with water, add some salt, and cook gently with the lid on for about 20 minutes, regularly skimming off any residue that collects on the top.

Fry the nuts in a frying pan with a little butter, and once golden brown, remove from the heat.

When the chicken is cooked, remove each piece from the stock (reserving the stock) and place in a roasting pan. Preheat the broiler to high.

Put the freekeh in a large saucepan over medium heat, then pour in enough of the chicken stock so that it is ½ inch/1 cm above the freekeh. It's best to use a sieve to strain out the cloves, cardamom, and cinnamon sticks (reserve the cinnamon for later). Allow the freekeh to simmer, with a lid on, for about 30 minutes, until cooked thoroughly and all the water has evaporated.

About 10 minutes before the freekeh is ready, broil the chicken for a couple of minutes to crisp it. If you think it may be too dry, add a couple of tablespoons of the chicken stock.

To serve, place the freekeh in a large serving bowl, add the reserved cinnamon sticks, place the chicken pieces on top, and sprinkle with the fried nuts and pomegranate seeds, if using. If you prefer your chicken in smaller pieces, you can shred if off the bone and mix it all together with the freekeh. Drizzle with olive oil.

Alternative:
You can also make this a nice salad: just pour in some olive oil, walnuts, and pomegranate molasses to taste, and mix well.

Chicken with Caramelized Onions and Sumac

(Msakhan)

This is traditionally a Palestinian dish that has made its way to Syria via the Palestinian refugees who fled their home country after the creation of Israel in 1948. We cooked this with Israa' (see page 132) and her mother, who are now refugees twice over and still carrying their traditions everywhere they go. The combination of sweet caramelized onions with the tang of sumac and chicken is just superb. It is mouthwateringly good and incredibly succulent, as the bread soaks up all the juices and flavors.

SERVES 6–8

½ cup/100 ml vegetable oil, divided

½ tablespoon black peppercorns

1 (4-pound/2 kg) chicken, cut up

2 pounds/1 kg onions, sliced

3 tablespoons sumac, plus extra for sprinkling

6 flatbreads or tortillas

Toasted pine nuts, to serve (optional)

Start by preparing the chicken. Heat a few tablespoons of the oil in a large pan and fry the peppercorns for a couple of minutes. Add the chicken pieces, fry for another minute, and then cover with a lid and cook over low heat for 20 to 30 minutes, turning occasionally until crispy on all sides.

Caramelize the onions in a pan with the rest of the oil over very low heat until they are completely soft and browned, about 30 minutes. Then add the sumac and simmer for about 5 minutes more.

Lay the bread on a large plate or tray and spread the caramelized onions all over. Place the chicken pieces on top and sprinkle with a bit more sumac and toasted pine nuts, if using.

Alternative:
You can also make mini wraps and serve them cold as part of a summer picnic. Simply shred the chicken, mix with the onions and sumac, and place in the middle of a tortilla, then roll up and cut into little finger-sized wraps.

Chicken in Tahini Sauce

(Fetteh Jaaj)

This is another fetteh dish, but this one is served for lunch or dinner, as it is heartier. The addition of chicken makes it more filling, and in another variation it is often bulked up with a layer of basmati rice, which makes it a complete meal in itself. Or you can serve it with rice on the side if you prefer.

This needs to be eaten fresh, so assemble when you're sure you are ready to eat.

SERVES 4

3 flatbreads

Vegetable oil, for coating and frying

1 cup/200 ml plain yogurt

2 garlic cloves, crushed

2 tablespoons tahini

Juice of 1 lemon

Salt and pepper, to taste

4 boneless chicken breasts

1 generous tablespoon butter, plus 1 tablespoon for topping

1 cup/200 g basmati rice

1½ cups/400 ml boiling water

1 cup/50 g chopped parsley

½ cup/75 g pomegranate seeds

Handful of toasted pine nuts or sliced almonds

Preheat the oven to 350°F/180°C. Start by coating the bread with some oil all over, then cut into small squares and bake in the oven until golden and crispy.

Prepare the sauce by combining the yogurt and garlic and whisking until smooth. Add the tahini while stirring rapidly, then add the lemon juice. Season with salt and pepper.

Fry the chicken breasts in a little oil, turning occasionally until they start to turn golden and are cooked through. Leave to cool, then shred into small pieces.

In a pot, melt the butter, then add the rice, season well with salt and pepper, and fry for a minute. Add the boiling water, reduce the heat, cover, and simmer for about 20 minutes, until the water has evaporated.

In a big serving dish, start assembling by evenly distributing the chicken and the rice. Top with the yogurt sauce and flatbread and finish by sprinkling on the parsley and pomegranate seeds. Fry the almonds in the remaining butter and add on top for extra richness.

Mona

In Beirut we met Mona, a kindhearted, beautiful, intelligent woman who lives in hope of one day returning to Damascus.

It was during Ramadan, on the 5th of August, 2012, that clashes intensified in Hameh and explosions were drawing nearer to Mona's house. Power had been cut off for two days and, as usual, they broke their fast by candlelight and ate breakfast to the sound of mortar shells.

It was a rough night for her five-year-old son, Bader, who had leukemia. He was bleeding from his mouth and nose,

blue spots covered his body, and his temperature was 105 degrees. Mona began to cry and said to her husband, "He needs to go to a hospital urgently." "How can we go?" he replied. "We don't have a car and no car will enter or leave Hameh while mortar shells are raining down."

That night, Mona's heart burned with worry for her son as she helplessly watched him twist in pain. All she could do was pray, wipe the blood from his face, and hold him until the light of day appeared. By morning she became impatient and told her husband,

"I won't wait another minute; I want to take him to the hospital even if I have to carry him myself and walk through the shelling."

She put on her headscarf and carried Bader outside. By complete coincidence, their neighbors were loading a minivan in preparation to flee the city. Mona and Bader squeezed into the van and were driven under shelling to the hospital. "The fear of dying under shellfire then turned into fear at the urgent shouting of the nurses as they took my son away and covered his face with an oxygen mask. I saw them rushing to help him. I saw him breathing with difficulty. I knew then he was dying. I called his father saying, 'If you don't come right away you will miss Bader forever.' He quickly arrived at the hospital for the doctor to tell us that the disease had spread all over Bader's body and that his lungs and heart had stopped responding. Bader died before his father's eyes and mine. His only obituary was a text message sent from his father's mobile. We went home and took Bader with us. It was his last trip back home."

Under the siege and clashes of Hameh, Bader's burial was quick. The family was advised to go in the smallest possible group to the burial because snipers on the other side would shoot at any gathering, even at a cemetery. Only five people went to bury him, among them his father, but not Mona. "Bader's tomb is without a stone, and I today feel as if I never said goodbye to him or buried him. I am tortured by one thought ever since we left Syria—I left my son behind."

The conflicts meant they were not able to give Bader a proper wake, where Mona could serve his favorite foods, such as Maqloubeh or stuffed zucchini. Mona wanted to share these dishes as a way of keeping her memory of him alive.

Rice and Eggplant
(Maqloubeh)

Maqloubeh means "turned over" in Arabic and that's exactly what this is—a big upside-down rice dish. It is beloved across the Middle East, and we've discovered the secret is in the stock—ideally homemade and full of spices (see page 247 for the best recipe). Don't be disappointed if, when you turn it upside down, the "cake" doesn't keep its shape, as it will still taste delicious.

While we were cooking, Mona (see page 128) told us this cute story about her son: "One day Bader came up to me and said, 'Mummy, why do we call Maqloubeh "Maqloubeh"?' I said, 'Once upon a time, a dish was walking down the street. It tripped and fell upside down on its face. Everyone gathered around and started eating it. Since that day, every time we cook it, we flip it upside down and eat it.' He looked at me with his big eyes and started laughing. He always used to ask me to cook this for him."

SERVES 4

2 eggplants, sliced into ½-inch/1 cm thick discs

Vegetable oil, for roasting and frying

2 large tomatoes, sliced into ½-inch/1 cm-thick discs

1 medium onion, sliced into ¼-inch/5 mm-thick discs

Salt, to taste

1¼ cups/250 g basmati rice

2 cups/500 ml chicken or vegetable stock (page 247)

2 bone-in, skin-on chicken drumsticks

2 bone-in, skin-on chicken thighs

Handful of toasted almonds

Plain yogurt, to serve (optional)

Fry the eggplant in vegetable oil in a skillet on both sides until browned and soft, then set on paper towels to drain. If you want a healthier option, preheat the oven to 350°F/180°C. Place the eggplant on a baking sheet, drizzle with a good amount of oil, and then roast for 35 minutes.

Layer the vegetables on the bottom of a saucepan; the eggplant first, then the tomatoes and onion. Season with salt, then scatter the rice evenly on top and pour in the stock. Bring to a boil, put a lid on, and turn the heat down to a simmer. It should take about 20 to 30 minutes for all the water to evaporate and the rice to cook through.

Meanwhile, shallow-fry the chicken in some oil. The skin should crisp up, and the pieces should be cooked through.

Uncover the rice, place a large flat platter on top of the pan, and then carefully turn it upside down, making sure you are holding the pan tightly. Top with the chicken and toasted almonds. Serve with plain yogurt, if you wish.

Israa'

Israa' is a feisty girl of twenty-four from Yarmouk, the Palestinian camp-turned-buzzing Damascus suburb, which was starved into submission by the government in 2014.

Israa' comes from a conservative family, but in her heart she is "free as a butterfly and as ambitious as Hillary Clinton." When we first met her, she took us by surprise with her impressive ability to express herself and her joie de vivre that turns every situation into a party. She loves makeup and fashion, and has written about both online.

When Israa' turned up in a neon green outfit at rehearsals for our theater project, the whole place was blown away. She is always in full makeup, has perfectly manicured nails, and wears high heels. She was wearing four-inch heels when she was forced to flee Syria—she walked in them for hours and hours on her way out of Yarmouk towards the Lebanese border. Israa' still keeps those shoes but has never worn them since. "They hurt too much," she said, "psychologically as well as physically."

But she's not the dainty food-avoider you'd imagine from her svelte, chic appearance. For Israa', food is a religion. Driving through Beirut in a taxi, she kept pointing at billboards, saying, "I wonder how you make that?" or "Yum, that looks delicious."

We got to talking about food stories from Yarmouk and, as she rifled through her memory bank, she suddenly beamed the broadest smile: "Pink fresh cakes!" she exclaimed. "Fresh cakes" are sinfully caloric, chemically colored small cakes. Little boys wake up early on a weekend morning and run to the bakery, where they pile huge trays with dozens of little square cakes and disperse throughout the alleys of Yarmouk, yelling to the residents to come and get 'em. Waking slowly to the shouts of the kids below in the street, followed swiftly by that early morning fresh-baked smell, the first cigarette, the tea brewing on the stove, Israa's sister would emerge bleary-eyed to join her. . . Rituals like these live long in the memory.

Israa' couldn't tell us how to actually make "fresh cakes," as she doesn't have all the right artificial colors and flavorings, but she and her mother cooked us something that we think is way more delicious—one of the most traditional Palestinian dishes, msakhan, accompanied by mendi, rice with a hint of smokiness.

Smoked Rice
(Mendi)

Mendi is originally from Yemen, and the huge spread of Yemeni restaurants in Syria in the years before the troubles has made this dish very popular. In Yemen, it is cooked underground using charcoal, which gives it its unique smokiness and cooks the chicken to perfection. As savvy Syrians wanted to cook it at home and achieve the same smokiness, they invented a much simpler smoking method that we learned from Israa' (see page 132). It's usually served with a hot salsa.

SERVES 4

For the stock

1 onion, quartered

1 tomato, quartered

Vegetable oil, for frying

10 cardamom pods, lightly crushed

4 bay leaves

½ teaspoon ground ginger

1 teaspoon ground coriander

1½ teaspoons ground turmeric

½ teaspoon ground nutmeg

8 cloves

1 pound/500 g bone-in, skin-on chicken thighs

6 cups/1½ L boiling water

For the salsa

1 onion

1 green bell pepper, seeded and roughly chopped

3 ripe tomatoes, cored

1 red cayenne or birdseye chile, seeds removed

Salt and pepper, to taste

For the rice

1 teaspoon butter or ghee

1 carrot, grated

2 heaped tablespoons sultanas

1½ cups/300 g basmati rice

1 piece of untreated charcoal

Handful of almonds or cashews

Butter or ghee, for frying

Plain yogurt, to serve (optional)

Make the chicken stock by quickly frying the onion and tomato in oil in a large saucepan, then adding the spices, chicken thighs, and the water. Bring to a boil and simmer for a good 30 minutes. Remove the chicken from the stock using a slotted spoon and set aside. Strain the stock, discarding the solids.

Make the salsa by blending the onion really well in a food processor. Add the pepper, tomatoes, chile, and salt and pepper, then blend well to make a rough sauce.

For the rice, heat the butter in a medium saucepan, then add the carrot, sultanas, and rice. Stir to coat in the butter for a minute before adding 2½ cups/600 ml of the reserved chicken stock, then simmer over low heat with the lid on until the rice is cooked through, about 20 minutes.

While the rice is cooking, fry or grill the reserved chicken to crisp the skin. When the rice is cooked, turn off the heat and use a spoon to make a hole in the middle of it. Pour some oil into a small heatproof bowl and place the bowl in the hole. Hold the piece of charcoal on an open flame, using metal tongs, and turn it in the flame to make sure it is completely hot on all sides. Then gently drop the charcoal into the bowl of oil and immediately put the lid back on. Leave the rice to rest for 5 minutes as the smoke infuses the rice.

Meanwhile, fry the nuts in a bit of butter or ghee.

Remove the bowl of charcoal. Spoon the rice out onto a large serving plate, place the chicken on top, sprinkle with the nuts, and serve with the salsa on the side. You can also serve with plain yogurt, if desired.

Whole Roast Chicken with Potatoes

(Jaaj bil Furn)

Crossing the Mediterranean in a dinghy was no easy decision for Tarik and Nisreen and their four children. They arrived in Samos in the middle of the night, wet and totally starving. There was a tiny shop open selling sliced meat. Tarik and his daughter Israa' went there and bought tons of it with fresh tomatoes and buns. They made sandwiches and all sat together on the pavement, sheltered under a parked truck and munched them up.

Nine months after their arduous journey, in a complex of flats outside Cologne, this was the first recipe they cooked for us. This is in honor of Israa's family and that day in Samos that they will never forget.

SERVES 4

For the chicken

3 tablespoons vegetable oil

1 teaspoon tomato paste

1 teaspoon red pepper paste
(page 242)

1 teaspoon freshly ground coriander

½ teaspoon ground cardamom

½ teaspoon ground nutmeg

½ teaspoon ground cumin

Generous amount of salt and pepper

1 whole chicken

3 onions, quartered

2 cups/500 ml water

For the potatoes

1½ pounds/750 g russet potatoes, thinly sliced

⅔ cup/150 ml water

Salt, to taste

Juice of 1 lemon

2 big garlic cloves, crushed into small pieces

1 teaspoon freshly ground coriander

Preheat the oven to 475°F/200°C. Mix the oil, tomato and red pepper pastes, coriander, cardamom, nutmeg, cumin, and salt and pepper. Place the chicken in a deep baking dish and rub it all over with the mixture. Add the onions and the water to the pan, then roast in the oven for 1 hour, or until the juices run clear.

Meanwhile, place the potato slices in a separate baking tray, add the water, and season with some salt. Roast in the oven with the chicken for the last 30 minutes of the cooking time. Combine the lemon juice, garlic, coriander, and salt to taste in a small bowl. Remove the potatoes from the oven, then drizzle with the lemon mixture and serve alongside the chicken.

Stuffed Cabbage

(Malfouf)

This is a great meal for autumn or winter, when cabbages are in season.

Pharmacist Razan (see page 194) told us that cumin is used in this dish because cabbage contains sulphur. Cumin apparently balances out the effects of that on the gut, as it has properties that aid digestion and eliminate flatulence. You learn something new every day! She also said that in Damascus they use white cabbage, but when she has tried it in the U.K. it doesn't cook that well, so she always uses green winter cabbages.

SERVES 4–6

1 green cabbage

6 ounces/150 g ground beef

1 cup/200 g short-grain rice

½ teaspoon ground cumin

1 teaspoon ground coriander

½ teaspoon 7 spices (page 244)

1 teaspoon salt

½ teaspoon black pepper

1 tablespoon olive oil

Bulb of garlic, broken into cloves (unpeeled)

Juice of 1 lemon

Trim off the large tough outer leaves of the cabbage and set to one side. Make four deep cuts around the core of the cabbage in order to make the leaves easier to pull off later. Leaving the cabbage whole, put it in a deep, large pot, with the core facing down, and pour a full kettle of boiling water over it—the cabbage should not be fully covered in water, just about halfway. Put a lid on and simmer over low heat until the cabbage leaves have softened, about 50 minutes. The idea is that the cabbage boils at the bottom and steams at the top. Take the pan off the heat but leave the cabbage in the pan with the lid on to continue steaming for a further 10 minutes or so.

Meanwhile, prepare the stuffing by putting the beef, rice, cumin, coriander, 7 spices, salt, pepper, and oil in a bowl and mixing well with your hands.

Remove the cabbage from the water and very gently pull off each leaf, always from the base to avoid tearing. You need to keep the leaves whole—if they don't want to come off, make the cuts deeper.

You are now ready to start stuffing and rolling. If the stalks are particularly large, gently cut them out (you can fry these later in butter). The size of the leaf will determine

how much stuffing you put in—it could be as little as
½ teaspoon, or as much as 1½ teaspoons. Be careful not
to overfill, though, as this will cause tearing later on. Place
the leaf sideways, so the spine is horizontal to you, and put
the stuffing in the middle, running along the spine like
a sausage shape, but leaving room at either side for folding.
Pinch the sides in first, then roll up into a parcel. Place in a
deep frying pan or stock pot, flap-side down, tightly packed,
and layer them with the unpeeled garlic cloves.

When the pan is full or you have used all the cabbage, place
the tough outer leaves over the top like a cover. Put a weighted
plate on top to prevent them from moving around, then
pour boiling water into the pan so that it comes to ½ inch/
1 cm above the plate. Simmer over low heat for about
50 minutes.

Drain off any remaining water, then place a larger plate over
the pan and carefully turn it over. If you're lucky, the rolls
will come out in the shape of the pan and look somewhat
like a cake! Squeeze lemon juice all over before serving.

The Stuffed Sheikh

(Sheikh Al Mahshi)

Once Mona (see page 128) had moved out of the refugee camp, she invited us to her new home in Beirut. Along with Mona and her four friends, we set about preparing a feast. After 20 minutes we heard a knock at the door; it was a man from Hezbollah checking we were not spies—he had seen us enter with cameras. Once he saw seven women preparing food, he left us to it, and the gossiping and cooking continued. We eventually sat down to this delicious meal of stuffed zucchini.

SERVES 4

For the stuffing

1½ pounds/700 g small pale green zucchini

1 onion, very finely chopped

1 tablespoon butter

1 tablespoon toasted pine nuts, plus extra to serve

8 ounces/250 g ground beef or lamb, or a combination of the two

Salt

Oil, for frying

For the sauce

2¾ cups/700 g plain yogurt

2½ cups/600 ml vegetable or chicken stock (page 247), cooled

1 egg

Chop the tops off the zucchini and core the centers with a corer. Be careful not to let the zucchini break. You can save the insides to use in the recipe on page 36.

Fry the onion in butter for about 5 minutes then add the pine nuts. Cook until the nuts turn golden, another 3 to 4 minutes.

Once the onions are soft, add the meat and season with salt, then fry until browned and cooked through. Let cool.

Stuff the zucchini with the meat mixture, making sure it is tightly packed. Use your finger to push the meat down.

Fry the zucchini in oil until all sides are slightly caramelized.

Meanwhile, pour the yogurt, stock, and egg into a blender and blend very well. Transfer to a pan and, over very low heat, slowly warm it, stirring constantly until it boils. If it curdles after heating, then blend again with an immersion or regular blender. Place the zucchini in the yogurt and simmer for about 10 minutes.

Serve the zucchini in the hot yogurt sauce in a large bowl and sprinkle with toasted pine nuts.

Vegetarian option:
Replace the meat with a mixture of roughly chopped nuts.

Baba Ganoush with Ground Lamb
(Batirsh)

This fancy version of baba ganoush is a specialty of Hama, a city north of Homs, famous for its waterwheels. Were you to ask anyone in Hama what their favorite dish is, they would probably very proudly say Batirsh. It is a rich tomato sauce and ground meat layered with baba ganoush. Some people cook the meat in the tomato sauce, and others like to cook it separately and have more layers in the dish.

It's normally served as a main and eaten with flatbread and fresh green peppers on the side.

SERVES 4-6

2 garlic cloves, crushed

1 teaspoon butter

1 pound/500 g tomatoes, blended

1 teaspoon salt

8 ounces/250 g ground lamb or beef

Oil, for frying

Smoked Eggplant Dip (page 40)

Handful of pine nuts, toasted

Small handful of parsley, finely chopped

Flatbread, to serve

Green bell peppers, sliced to serve (optional)

Fry the garlic in a pan with the butter until they soften, then add the tomatoes and salt and simmer for approximately 30 minutes until reduced.

In a separate pan, fry the meat in a bit of oil until it browns and is cooked through. If you want to combine the meat and tomato layers, add the meat to the tomatoes and reduce together.

Put the eggplant dip in a large, shallow bowl, layer the tomato sauce on top, then add the meat and sprinkle with the pine nuts and parsley. Serve with flatbread and peppers, if using.

Deep-Fried Kibbeh and Kibbeh in Hot Yogurt Sauce

(Kibbeh Maqliyeh and Kibbeh Labaniyeh)

If you want to show your guests that you care, you give them kibbeh, perhaps *the* signature dish of the Levant. Anything mixed and kneaded with bulgur wheat counts as kibbeh; you'll see a lot of different varieties in the region in all sorts of flavors, shapes, and sizes.

Deep-fried kibbeh balls stuffed with ground meat and served with heaps of yogurt on the side are a real treat for the whole family. Many of the women we met don't have food processors to blend the bulgur, meat, and spices, so the local butchers mix it for them.

For the stuffing

Vegetable oil, for deep-frying

1 onion, peeled and quartered

4 ounces/100 g ground beef

¾ cup/75 g pine nuts

1 teaspoon dried marjoram

½ teaspoon ground cumin

½ teaspoon black pepper

Salt

For the dough

⅔ cup/100 g fine bulgur wheat

1 onion, peeled and quartered

4 ounces/100 g ground beef

1½ teaspoons dried marjoram

1 teaspoon ground cumin

½ teaspoon 7 spices (page 244)

½ teaspoon black pepper

Salt

For the yogurt sauce

3 cups/750 g plain yogurt

2½ cups/600 ml vegetable or chicken stock (page 247), cooled

1 egg

Rice or bulgur wheat, to serve

Start by making the stuffing: heat a bit of oil in a frying pan and slowly fry the onion over low heat until it starts to caramelize, then add the meat, pine nuts, marjoram, cumin, pepper, and salt to taste and continue to cook until the meat has browned. Remove from the heat and allow to cool.

To make the dough, blend the onion in a food processor, then add the meat, marjoram, cumin, 7 spices, pepper, and salt and blend until it forms a thick paste. Remove and put in a large mixing bowl.

Rinse and drain the bulgur and leave to one side to absorb the excess water.

Blend the bulgur briefly in the food processor before adding it to the meat mixture. Knead everything together really well with your hands and leave to one side while you make the stuffing.

To make the kibbeh, take a bit of the dough mixture and roll it into a ball, slightly smaller than a ping pong ball. Put your forefinger in the middle of the ball and carve out a hole while rotating the ball with your other hand. You want to try to get the exterior as thin as possible without tearing it. Put 1 to 2 teaspoons of the stuffing into the hole and seal it over by bringing the dough over the hole. It helps to have a bowl of water near you to use to smooth over the outer edge. Make into a football shape with two little pointed ends.

Fill a pan halfway with vegetable oil and heat until almost boiling, then drop a few kibbeh in to deep-fry in batches. When they are dark brown and crispy, remove them with a slotted spoon and place on paper towels until you are ready to serve.

If you want to turn your kibbeh into a main course, mix the yogurt, stock, and egg in a blender until thoroughly combined. Heat the sauce in a large saucepan, over very low heat, stirring constantly until it boils. If it curdles, blend again. Pour over the kibbeh and serve hot with rice or bulgur on the side.

Old Man's Ears

(Shishbarak)

We worked on this dish with four women who were living in the Shatila camp. Six of us sat around gossiping, kneading, rolling, and stuffing, while one of their daughters was in the kitchen heating and constantly stirring the yogurt, learning the tricks of the trade.

We found an old recipe for Shishbarak in a fifteenth-century Arabic cookbook, and today you can find versions of it in almost every country that was once part of the Persian empire. The Syrian name evolved from the ancient Iranian word *joshpara*, which then became *joshepara*, meaning "lamb's ear." It gets an even funnier nickname in Syria—Old Man's Ears—partly because the dumplings are made into ear shapes.

If you don't have time to make your own dough, you can buy ready-made dumpling wrappers from any Asian shop. They should come in a pack of one hundred individual portions.

For the dough

4 cups/500 g all-purpose flour, plus extra for dusting

Pinch of salt

For the stuffing

2 to 3 onions, finely chopped

3 tablespoons vegetable oil

1 pound/500 g ground lamb or beef, or a mix of the two

½ teaspoon ground coriander

½ teaspoon ground cumin

¼ teaspoon ground turmeric

½ teaspoon ground black pepper

¼ teaspoon ground nutmeg

1 teaspoon salt

For the yogurt

3 cups/750 g plain yogurt

2½ cups/600 ml vegetable or chicken stock (page 247), cooled

1 egg

For the topping

3 garlic cloves, crushed

Handful of fresh cilantro, finely chopped

1 teaspoon butter

2 tablespoons/10 g pine nuts, toasted

In a large bowl, mix the flour and a pinch of salt, adding water gradually until you have the beginnings of a dough. If it's too sticky, add a bit more flour; if too dry, add a drop more water. Knead the dough for a good 10 minutes, then transfer to a bowl, cover with a kitchen towel, and leave for 10 to 15 minutes.

Meanwhile, make the stuffing. Caramelize the onions in the oil over a low heat, for about 30 minutes, then add the meat, coriander, cumin, turmeric, pepper, nutmeg, and salt. Continue to fry until the meat is cooked, then pour into a bowl and leave to cool.

Sprinkle some flour onto a clean work surface and roll the dough out, about ⅛ inch/3 mm thick. Using a 2-inch/ 5-cm pastry cutter or a glass, cut out circles. Keep going until you have used up all the dough.

The meat should have cooled down by now, so you can start making your little parcels. Take a circle of the dough (you may need to stretch it out a bit), put a teaspoon or thereabouts of the meat in the middle, fold it in half and then, using your fingertips, press the edges together, so that it makes a tight semicircle shape. Take each corner of the semicircle and bring them together, making a little round parcel.

Mix the yogurt, stock, and egg in a blender until thoroughly combined. Heat the yogurt sauce in a large saucepan, over very low heat, stirring constantly until it boils. If it curdles, blend again.

Once it starts to boil, gently drop the dumplings in and, after about 10 minutes, check if they are ready by cutting one in half. If the dough is still soft, give them a bit longer.

Lightly fry the garlic and cilantro in a bit of butter for 1 minute until they are aromatic and the cilantro has wilted.

Pour the dumplings and sauce into a large bowl and sprinkle with toasted pine nuts and the fried garlic and cilantro.

Cherry Kebab
(Kebab al Karaz)

Cherry kebab is the epitome of luxury—the kind of dish you can imagine a rich Venetian merchant feasting on during a visit to ancient Aleppo. Whenever we visited Aleppo before the war, we'd make sure to seek out this dish at one of the Old City's legendary Arabic house restaurants. It is a huge treat, a bit like having your main course and your dessert all in one. This is not a kebab in the Turkish sense, but in the Syrian sense. It is traditionally made with the sour black cherries that grow on the outskirts of the city and is only eaten when they are in season. Using canned black cherries is a cheaper option and means you can make it all year round. Cherry kebab is usually served on flatbread, but it's also great with rice.

SERVES 2–4

1 small onion, very finely chopped or blended in a food processor

2 handfuls of parsley, very finely chopped, plus extra to serve

1 pound/500 g ground lamb

2½ teaspoons salt

1 teaspoon black pepper

1½ pounds/750 g fresh or canned black cherries, pitted and quartered

4 tablespoons pomegranate molasses

2 tablespoons lemon juice

1½ teaspoons ground cinnamon

Vegetable oil, for roasting

4 flatbreads, to serve

½ cup/50 g pine nuts, toasted

Preheat the oven to 350°F/180°C. In a large bowl, mix the onion, parsley, lamb, salt, and black pepper by hand. Take handfuls of the mixture and mold it into 1-inch/2.5 cm-round balls—keep a bowl of water close by and regularly wet your hands, as this will give them a smooth finish.

Place the cherries in a large pan with 2 cups/500 ml of water (only if using fresh cherries; if using canned cherries, add cherries and their liquid), the pomegranate molasses, lemon juice, and cinnamon. Bring to a boil and then simmer for around 30 minutes. Stir frequently, squashing some of the cherries for flavor and to thicken the sauce.

Meanwhile, place the meatballs on a baking tray and drizzle with oil. Roast in the oven for 4 minutes, turning occasionally. Be careful not to overcook them. When done, add any juices from the baking tray to the cherries for a richer sauce.

When the sauce is thick but not gooey, add the meatballs and simmer for another 4 minutes. Meanwhile, cut the bread into triangles and lay out on a large tray or plate. Pour the cherry kebab on top. Sprinkle with toasted pine nuts and chopped parsley.

Shaima

Shaima's best food memories of her hometown, Raqqa, are of eating Syrian-style ice cream in a shop located on what was then called the Square of Heaven. "In summer my brother would take us there every evening. We would buy ice cream and sit on the grass. It used to be all hustle and bustle, lights and laughter and children playing around." Shaima is now "internally displaced" in southern Syria; she picks apples to earn a living and eats one a day herself. "It is good for my skin," she told us.

Shaima was orphaned at age six and raised by her brother and his wife, and when she got married her life was no easier. She never believed in wearing the hijab, but after the wedding her husband forced her to wear one. Worse than that, her new in-laws thought she was too skinny to be considered a real woman, so they convinced her to take cortisone pills to put on weight. She took them for three months, which caused her to expand like a balloon and feel constantly ill.

In 2015 Shaima escaped both ISIS and her husband and went back to live with her brother. Today, the Square of Heaven no longer sells ice creams— it has become ISIS's preferred location for public beheadings. The locals now call it the Square of Hell.

Okra and Lamb Stew

(Bamia)

Shaima's favorite dish is okra stew. It is actually a much-loved dish in the Euphrates area, as okra is widely cultivated there. Shaima joked once that "if they analyzed my blood, they would find okra cells" because she eats so much of it. When Dina was a child, this stew was her favorite dish. She loved finding the tasty white things, which she learned later were the garlic cloves!

SERVES 4

1 teaspoon butter

1 pound/500 g lamb cubes, from the leg or the shoulder

½ teaspoon ground nutmeg

½ teaspoon 7 spices (page 244)

Salt and pepper, to taste

8 garlic cloves

1 pound/500 g ripe tomatoes, blended

1 (14-ounce/400 g) can chopped tomatoes

1 tablespoon tomato paste

1⅔ cups/400 ml boiling water

20 ounces/570 g okra, fresh or frozen

Plain basmati rice, to serve

Heat the butter in a deep pan and fry the lamb until it turns brown all over. Add the nutmeg and 7 spices, then season with the salt and pepper. Add the garlic and fry for another minute or so.

Add the fresh tomatoes, canned tomatoes, and tomato paste. Top with boiling water and simmer over low heat for 35 minutes.

If you are using fresh okra, trim the ends. Add the okra to the stew and simmer for a further 25 minutes, or until the okra is soft and the tomato sauce has thickened.

Serve with basmati rice.

Kibbeh in Tray
(Kibbeh bil Siniyeh)

If you are making a huge amount of kibbeh, it can end up being laboriously time-consuming, but as they are an important part of Syrian cuisine you really ought to give it a try. An easier method is to bake them in a tray rather than as individual deep-fried balls.

We made this with a lady called Saalha, who was adamant that this tray of baked kibbeh is immeasurably superior to the individual balls, not to mention healthier and easier to make. Eat it with minted yogurt and a lemony tomato and cucumber salad.

For the dough

1 onion, peeled and quartered

7 ounces/200 g ground beef

1 teaspoon ground cumin

1 teaspoon 7 spices (page 244)

1 teaspoon dried marjoram

1⅓ cups/200 g fine brown bulgur wheat, rinsed and drained

Salt, to taste

For the stuffing

1 onion, peeled and quartered

Vegetable oil, for frying

10 ounces/300 g ground lamb or beef

¼ teaspoon ground cumin

¼ teaspoon 7 spices (page 244)

¼ teaspoon dried marjoram

2 cups/100 g walnut halves, very finely chopped

2 tablespoons pomegranate molasses

Salt and pepper, to taste

Handful of pine nuts, for topping

For the yogurt

2 cups/500 g plain yogurt

2 Persian cucumbers, diced

Dried mint, to taste

Preheat the oven to 350°F/180°C and grease a 9-inch/23 cm springform cake pan.

First make the dough. In a food processor, finely blend the onion, then put it in a bowl with the meat, cumin, 7 spices, and marjoram. Blend the bulgur in the food processor before adding it to the bowl, then mix all the ingredients together using your hands, until it forms a nice thick dough. Leave to rest while you make the stuffing.

For the stuffing, fry the onion in a little oil until softened, then add the meat, cumin, 7 spices, and marjoram and continue to fry until the meat is completely brown and cooked through. Take off the heat, stir in the walnuts and pomegranate molasses, and season with salt and pepper.

To assemble the kibbeh, take half the dough mixture and pat it down in the cake pan so that it is evenly spread and smooth all over. Then evenly spread the stuffing mixture on top and cover with the rest of the dough. You can do this in two ways, by using a little bit of dough and pressing it down with your fingers, then adding a bit more and smoothing it out, eventually creating a whole layer that is smooth and even. Or spread it all out on some plastic wrap and press it down to form one large, thin layer that you can then gently invert on top.

Once you have formed your layers of dough and stuffing and it has a smooth top, score it with a knife in the pattern you wish (this will help when cutting it later), put the pine nuts on top, and bake in the oven for 30 to 40 minutes.

Make a yogurt dip by mixing the yogurt, diced cucumbers, and dried mint together and serve alongside the kibbeh.

Chicken in Turmeric Yogurt
(Mleheyya)

This is the favored local dish of Sweida and Dera'a, two cities in the Hauran region, about a one-hour drive south of Damascus.

Among members of the Druze sect of Sweida, there is a whole range of songs about this dish and its serving traditions. Two burly men carry the copper tray of food into the party and everyone sings, "Tuck into the food, tuck in, you knights, you honor us and make us feel at home." To show how generous the host is, ghee is then poured over the dish in huge quantities with great ceremony, and the girls sing, "Come on, soldier daughters! Pour the hot ghee 'til it's foamy!"

In Sweida the traditions of making mleheyya are just as sacred as the eating of it. The night before a wedding, the relatives of the groom—men and women—come together and stay up all night braising meat until it falls off the bone, cooking huge batches of bulgur wheat and brewing the broth that must be constantly stirred and watched. Most importantly, you mustn't forget the singing and celebration while you do it. By the time the guests arrive, a few trays of mleheyya should be ready to eat. Groups of guests gather around and collectively eat from the same tray. It's one of the nicest rituals by which Middle Eastern eating brings people together. We skipped the hot ghee to keep it healthier, but you can always add a bit at the end.

SERVES 6

Vegetable oil, for frying

3 medium-sized onions, sliced

1 pound/500 g potatoes, peeled and diced

½ cup/100 ml water

4 boneless, skinless chicken breasts, diced

Salt and pepper, to taste

Cooked bulgur wheat, to serve

For the turmeric yogurt sauce

3½ cups/800 g plain yogurt

3 cups/700 ml good-quality stock

1 egg

1½ heaped teaspoons ground turmeric

Heat a bit of oil in a frying pan and fry the onions over medium heat for 15 minutes, or until starting to caramelize. Add the potatoes and water, cover, and boil for 10 minutes, then add the chicken, season, and cook for a further 5 to 8 minutes.

Meanwhile, in a blender mix the yogurt, stock, and egg very well. Pour into a pan, place over very low heat, and keep stirring in one direction until the mixture boils. The constant stirring is essential here, as it will keep the yogurt from curdling. Add the turmeric and boil for a further minute or so.

Add the potatoes and chicken mixture to the yogurt, then boil together for 5 minutes.

Serve the stew on a bed of bulgur wheat.

Mixed Grill

(Meshwi)

Syrians love a barbecue. The weather's almost always good and there's no restriction on where you can light a fire and grill meat, so you see people doing it everywhere—on the side of the road, in the middle of a roundabout, by the motorway, and in the park. Any open space will do—on a warm evening in Damascus you usually see families sitting on the side of a road grilling and smoking argilla (sheesha pipe), with kids playing, unfazed by the traffic and surrounding noise. Some people play loud music as well. The streets become a chaotic communal party every day of the summer.

Place a metal grilling rack over two stones with charcoal underneath, and that's all you need to start making the juiciest meat dishes you can imagine. Beef or veal ribs are one of the most popular cuts. You can grill any cut of chicken, and for lamb, the neck or shoulder is the best. It is important for Syrians to include big pieces of pure fat and vegetables in the mix, as the fat keeps the meat juicy and seeps into the vegetables, giving them that divine taste you're looking for. These grilled meats and chicken are usually eaten with flatbread brushed with pepper paste and thinly sliced onion mixed with parsley and sumac.

SERVES 4

For the beef kebabs

½ onion, quartered

A handful of parsley

8 ounces/250 g ground fatty beef

1 teaspoon salt

7 spices, to taste (page 244)

¼ teaspoon pomegranate
molasses

For the lamb skewers

8 ounces/250 g diced lamb
leg or shoulder

Salt and pepper

5 small green bell peppers,
seeded and cut into chunks

2 small onions, quartered

4 tomatoes, quartered

For the chicken skewers

3 teaspoons oil

3 garlic cloves, crushed

½ teaspoon 7 spices (page 244)

¼ teaspoon ground cardamom

Salt, to taste

2 boneless, skinless chicken
breasts, diced

1 small onion, quartered

1 tomato, quartered

5 baby green peppers

Preheat the oven to 400°F/200°C. First make the beef kebabs. In a food processor, mix the onion with the parsley. Pour into a bowl with the ground meat, add salt, 7 spices, molasses, and mix everything together with your hands. Form the beef around metal skewers, then roast in the oven for 8 minutes or grill for 4 minutes on each side.

For the lamb skewers, season the lamb pieces with salt and pepper, then thread them onto metal skewers, alternating with pieces of pepper, onion, and tomato. Season and then grill or broil for 4 minutes on each side.

For the chicken skewers, mix the oil, garlic, 7 spices, cardamom, and some salt in a bowl. Add the chicken and the remaining vegetables and mix. Thread the chicken and vegetables onto metal skewers and grill for 4 minutes on each side.

Meatballs in a Tomato and Pepper Stew
(Dawood Pasha)

"Pasha" was once one of the highest ranks in the elaborate hierarchy of the Ottoman Empire, so this dish is all about exclusivity and luxury. *Dawood* means "David," so the recipe name translates as something like "Lord David." Apparently this dish was named after one particular Lord David, Dawood Pasha, who was governor in the Levant in the nineteenth century and loved this dish so much it became his signature. For all this grandeur, though, the recipe itself is actually simple and makes a great weekday supper with friends. It also keeps really well, and we find it is often more delicious the next day. Serve it with plain rice for a filling main course.

SERVES 4

For the sauce

1 onion, finely diced

Vegetable oil, for frying

5 garlic cloves, chopped

1 green bell pepper, seeded and diced

1 pound/500 g tomatoes, finely diced

2 tablespoons tomato paste

For the meatballs

1 pound/500 g ground lamb

1 onion, very finely chopped

1 pound/500 g ground lamb

½ large bunch of parsley, finely chopped

1 teaspoon 7 spices (page 244)

Salt, as needed

Olive oil, for drizzling

Cooked plain bulgur wheat or rice, to serve

Preheat the oven to 320°F/160°C.

For the sauce, fry the onion in a bit of oil until soft, then add the garlic and fry for a minute or two longer. Add the green pepper and tomatoes, then fry for a couple of minutes before turning the heat down to simmer for around 10 minutes. Stir in the tomato paste and continue to simmer for a further 30 minutes or so, until the tomatoes have reduced.

For the meatballs, mix the lamb, onion, parsley, 7 spices, and salt in a bowl and mold into balls about 1 inch/ 2.5 cm in diameter. Have a bowl of water handy to dip your fingers into to help you create a smooth edge on the meatballs. Place them on a baking tray lined with parchment paper, drizzle olive oil over them, and bake for 4 minutes.

Take the meatballs out of the oven and add them and their juices to the tomatoes, which by now should have reduced to a nice thick sauce. Leave to simmer for another 4 to 5 minutes, then take off the heat and serve with plain rice.

Eggplant and Lamb Kebabs
(Maldoum)

Maldoum is one of what seems like a hundred recipes we've come across that revolves around the magical combination of eggplant and ground meat. Every region in Syria has a slightly different name for it and its own particular technique. Whether it is sheikh mahshi, mnazaalla, or karin yarik, they all have almost the same ingredients, but to the eye of the connoisseur there are subtle differences in the way they are cooked. We tried them all out and distilled the best of them into the recipe below.

SERVES 4

4 medium eggplants

2 baking potatoes

Vegetable oil, for roasting

2 green bell peppers, seeded

4 medium tomatoes, blended

1 tablespoon tomato paste

A bunch of parsley, very finely chopped

2 tablespoons pomegranate molasses

½ teaspoon ground cumin

½ teaspoon 7 spices (page 244)

1 pound/500 g fatty ground lamb

Salt and pepper, to taste

Cooked bulgur wheat or rice, to serve

Heat the oven to 400°F/200°C.

Cut the eggplants in half lengthwise, then slice into discs. Slice the potatoes into discs, then place in separate oven trays and drizzle with a good amount of oil and a sprinkle of salt. Bake in the oven for 40 minutes until tender.

Meanwhile, cut the peppers into big chunks and set aside. Place the blended tomatoes and tomato paste in a pan over low heat and reduce for around 30 minutes. Season with salt and pepper.

Mix the parsley, pomegranate molasses, cumin, and 7 spices with the lamb and mix well before dividing into ½-inch/1 cm-thick round patties. Season with salt and pepper.

In a baking dish, pour in the tomato sauce, then start assembling the eggplant, potatoes, meat patties, and peppers in rows one after the other. Bake in the oven for 12 minutes and serve with bulgur or rice.

Rice with Lamb and Peas

(Ouzi)

Ouzi is another one of those dishes that Syrians tend to reserve for big occasions, like weddings. The rice is served on huge trays topped (if you really want to show off) with a whole lamb, roasted on hot stones in a pit in the desert, or, more realistically, with a choice cut that has been slow-roasted in the oven. It takes a little while to cook, but the preparation is a cinch. Yogurt is essential with this dish, served on the side and sprinkled with sumac and drizzled with olive oil.

SERVES 4–6

For the lamb

4 tablespoons yogurt

2 heaped teaspoons ground cumin

1 teaspoon ground coriander

1 teaspoon ground nutmeg

Generous amount of salt and pepper

3 tablespoons/45 ml vegetable oil

8 garlic cloves, crushed

1 whole bone-in leg of lamb (4½ to 5½ pounds/2 to 2.5kg)

5 onions, quartered

2 cups/500 ml water

For the rice

1 onion, diced

1 large carrot, diced

1 teaspoon butter

1½ cups/300 g basmati rice

3 cups/700 ml vegetable or chicken stock (page 247) or water

Salt and pepper, to taste

4 ounces/100 g frozen peas

Preheat the oven to 400°F/200°C.

First prepare the lamb. Mix the yogurt with the cumin, coriander, nutmeg, salt and pepper, oil, and garlic. Place the lamb in a deep baking pan, make a few scores into the meat, then rub with the yogurt sauce to coat all over. Add the onions and water to the pan, then cover tightly with foil and roast for 3 to 3½ hours, until the meat is falling off the bone.

Towards the end of the cooking time, make the rice. Fry the onion and carrot in some butter until they start to soften. Add the rice, stock, salt, and a good amount of pepper, then mix well. Bring to a boil, cover, and reduce the heat and simmer for 15 to 20 minutes, or until the water is absorbed. Stir in the frozen peas and cook for another 5 minutes.

White Bean and Lamb Stew

(Aisha Khanoum)

This dish literally means "Lady Aisha" and is apparently so-called because Lady Aisha, the wife of the Iranian Shah Nassir-Aldin Al Qajar, loved it so much that it came to be named after her. This is really hearty comfort food, perfect for breaking your Ramadan fast or for a cold winter night inside. It is fundamentally the same concept as baked beans but much fresher and more subtle. If you are vegetarian, just omit the meat.

SERVES 4

1 medium onion

Vegetable oil, for frying

5 garlic cloves, halved

1⅓ pounds/600 g ripe tomatoes, blended

2 cups/500 ml vegetable or chicken stock (page 247)

1 cup/200 g dried cannellini beans, soaked overnight and drained

2 heaped tablespoons tomato paste

Salt and pepper, to taste

8 lamb chops

A big bunch of parsley, chopped

Cooked plain rice or bulgur wheat, to serve

Fry the onion in a deep pan with the oil, over medium–low heat, for about 10 minutes. Add the garlic and continue to fry for a couple more minutes.

Add the tomatoes, stock, beans, tomato paste, salt, and pepper. Bring to a boil, then turn the heat down and simmer for around 90 minutes with the lid on, stirring occasionally.

Toward the end of the 90 minutes, sear the lamb chops over high heat for 4 minutes on each side.

Once the beans are tender and the sauce has become rich, turn off the heat, add the parsley, and serve alongside the lamb with rice or bulgur.

Spiced Fish
(Samaka Harra)

The beautiful coastal city of Latakia hasn't been without its troubles since the Syrian civil war broke out in 2011; since then it has been a site of protest activities and military restrictions limiting movement in and out of the city. But despite that, it is still considered a safer place to be than Damascus, Homs, or Aleppo, in each of which huge swathes of the city have been utterly annihilated, so many Syrians have moved to Latakia for a relatively safer life.

Of course, with coastal life comes coastal cuisine, so fish is obviously a much more common addition to the dinner table in these parts of the country. This oven-baked whole fish is packed with flavors, and when Fedwa (see page 175) suddenly pulled it out of her oven, we were not only impressed but very pleasantly surprised. It was juicy, crispy, and luscious all at the same time.

SERVES 2

6 garlic cloves, chopped

2 red cayenne or birdseye chiles, finely chopped

½ teaspoon ground cumin

½ cup/40 g walnuts, chopped

2 tablespoons olive oil, plus extra for drizzling

Salt and pepper, to taste

2 whole medium-sized fish, such as sea bream or snapper

1 bunch of fresh cilantro, roughly chopped, including the stems

1 lemon, halved, plus ½ lemon, sliced

Preheat the oven to 350°F/180°C.

In a bowl, mix together the garlic, chiles, cumin, walnuts, 2 tablespoons of olive oil, salt, and pepper.

Stuff the fish with this mix, reserving 2 tablespoons for later, then add a handful of cilantro, saving some to garnish.

Squeeze the lemon halves over both fish, then add a drizzle of olive oil and some salt and pepper. Leave in the fridge to marinate for a good half an hour.

Place the fish on a large oven tray with the rest of the stuffing on top and a couple of slices of lemon each, then bake in the oven for 30 minutes, or until the fish flakes easily.

Fedwa

Fedwa was a mother of five two years ago, but since then she has lost two of her sons—one to an accident at sea in Beirut, the other to a sniper's bullet in Yarmouk, the Palestinian suburb where they lived in Damascus. We met her in the kitchen of her flat on the third floor of an unfinished concrete block in Burj Al Barajneh, one of Beirut's long-standing Palestinian ghettos. It is "as small as the happiness in my heart," she said, but there she manages to produce an array of dishes that rarely fail to delight.

Fedwa is one of thousands of double refugees who fled Palestine as a child, only to be forced to flee again by the Syrian war. Yet cooking with her was really eye-opening because of the extra dimension that her travels have given to her cooking. She cooks mutabal, but with chard, and she is a living example of how the topsy-turvy politics of the Middle East are still producing cultural fusion and creativity, even if at heartbreaking human cost.

We've never seen Fedwa cook just one thing for supper; she always surprises us with a feast. If she is inviting people over, which she loves to do as often as possible, she will spend two days preparing—coring vegetables, rolling vine leaves, and soaking chickpeas. Canned food has no place in her kitchen.

We asked Fedwa what food means to her, and she replied, "When my son decided to move to Saudi Arabia with his wife, the first thing I worried about was how he was going to get a proper Syrian meal. So, the week before he left, I went on a mission, preparing supplies to keep him going for the first few months. I filled bag after bag with labneh balls, crammed jars with makdous, dried mint leaves, and mloukhia. I packed him jars of homemade tomato paste and grape molasses, pickled a few jars of olives, and God knows what more. The money he paid for extra luggage was so much more expensive than the food itself, but it was Syrian and made by me."

The Fisherman's Catch
(Sayadiyeh)

Sayadiyeh literally means the "fisherman's catch." It is a dish that is mainly made in the coastal cities of Latakia and Tartus, but Palestine, Lebanon, and Iraq have their versions of it too.

Avid host and cook Fedwa (see page 175) was constantly inviting us for lunch at her flat. Each time we visited she cooked us a different dish; this was possibly our favorite and, as we found out while eating, it was her children's favorite too. She turned a huge pan of it upside down onto a large tray and, just before serving, poured a load of melted ghee on top. "It makes it taste better and look shiny," she insisted. Here is her recipe minus the ghee—but feel free to smother it in ghee or butter if you like.

2 garlic cloves, crushed

Zest of 1 lemon

1 tablespoon olive oil

1 teaspoon salt, plus more to taste

1 heaped teaspoon ground ginger

½ teaspoon grated nutmeg

1 heaped teaspoon ground cumin

1 heaped teaspoon ground coriander

1 heaped teaspoon ground cardamom

4 white fish fillets, about 4 ounces/120 g each, such as haddock, cod, or sea bream

Vegetable oil, for frying

3 medium onions, thinly sliced

½ cup/100 g sultanas

1½ cups/300 g basmati rice, rinsed

2 cups/500 ml boiling water

Handful of almonds, toasted

Crush the garlic and salt with a mortar and pestle, then add lemon zest and olive oil. In a separate bowl, combine the ginger, nutmeg, cumin, coriander, and cardamom. Mix well, then add half the spice mixture to the garlic mixture. Rub the spiced garlic on the fish. Marinate in the fridge for 20 minutes.

In a frying pan with a little vegetable oil, caramelize the onions over low heat—it should take about 30 minutes. Then put half of them to one side for later and transfer half to a saucepan. Keep the frying pan and any oil from the onions for later.

Add the reserved spice mixture to the onions in the saucepan and fry for 2 to 3 minutes. Add the sultanas and cook for a couple of minutes before adding the rice. Ensure that the rice is coated in the spices and add the boiling water, then some salt. Allow to simmer over low heat with the lid on until all the water has evaporated and the rice is tender and fluffy.

Meanwhile, fry the fish for 3 minutes on each side over medium heat in the same frying pan you cooked the onions in.

Turn the rice out onto a tray or large plate and put the fish on top, then top with the reserved caramelized onions and the toasted almonds.

Fish in Tahini
(Samak bi Tahina)

It isn't only vegetables and meat that get smothered in tahini sauce in Syria.

White fish, such as red mullet and snapper, are commonly caught and eaten in the coastal towns. You don't want to mess too much with fresh fish, but this tahini sauce is one classic way to spice it up. Some people deep-fry the fish before putting it in the sauce, but we found that shallow-frying it is actually nicer and keeps it tasting fresh. This recipe goes really well with bulgur wheat and a side vegetable, such as Roasted Cauliflower with Cumin (page 23) or Chard with Garlic and Lemon (page 47).

SERVES 2

For the fish
½ teaspoon ground cumin
¼ teaspoon ground Aleppo pepper
½ teaspoon salt
1 teaspoon olive oil
2 fillets any white fish
2 medium onions, sliced
Vegetable oil, for frying

For the sauce
⅓ cup/80 ml tahini
⅓ cup/80 ml water
3 tablespoons/45 ml lemon juice
1 garlic clove, crushed
Salt and pepper, to taste

For the topping
1 garlic clove, chopped
Handful of cilantro, chopped
Handful of pine nuts, toasted

Cooked bulgur wheat or rice, to serve

Mix the cumin, Aleppo pepper, and salt with the oil and coat the fish with it, then leave to marinate in the fridge for 30 minutes.

Caramelize the onions by frying them in a pan with a little vegetable oil on the lowest heat until they turn brown and wilted—it should take about 30 minutes. Set aside for the topping.

Make the tahini sauce by mixing the tahini, water, lemon juice, garlic, salt, and pepper in a pan off the heat. Don't worry if it curdles at first, just keep stirring it rapidly. Warm the tahini sauce over very low heat.

Fry the marinated fish in vegetable oil in a large frying pan over medium heat for about 3 minutes on each side. Take off the heat and put the fish in a serving dish.

Next, prepare the rest of the topping. Fry the garlic and cilantro in a pan with some oil for 1 minute.

Pour the tahini sauce over the fish, add the onions on top, followed by the fried cilantro, garlic, and pine nuts.

Serve with bulgur or rice.

Sweets

If alcohol is the drug of choice in Europe, sugar and caffeine are Syria's addictions. As far as Syrians are concerned, the best thing to go with one sweet dish is another. On rare occasions Syrians even indulge in a double dessert treat for breakfast. In Aleppo, for instance, the traditional dish on a Friday morning is Qatayef (page 182) dipped in Mamounyya—a deep-fried pancake stuffed with clotted cream, covered in sugar syrup, and dipped in a sweet semolina cinnamon pudding. So look away now if you're watching your waistline!

By "sweets" we mean the little treats that you give to guests who aren't staying for supper but are just visiting for an afternoon tea; the delicious morsels in shop windows that kids lust after; and also what you might call dessert.

Sweet Stuffed Pancakes
(Qatayef)

Qatayef have been described as the "joys of heaven" and have often been written about in verse as objects of love and desire. They are the most mentioned of all the sweets in the *Arabian Nights* tales. The root of the word *qatayef* is "qatifa," which means "plush, velvet." Even Rumi, the greatest of the Persian poets, eulogized them: "the palate ease and the throat they please."

During Ramadan, you can hardly find a corner of Damascus where there isn't some guy making these delicacies outside on a flat saj (a domed convex grill that is usually used to make a special kind of thin flatbread).

We met Saalha in Beirut, who taught us an array of recipes all in one day, including these. They were so delicious that we ate them before the main course was ready! When eaten hot from the pan they are unbelievably scrumptious. You can stuff the pancakes with nuts, curd, or both. They are best served warm, but be careful not to eat them before the main course!

MAKES 8

1 ½ cups/200 g all-purpose flour

½ teaspoon instant yeast

½ teaspoon granulated sugar

½ teaspoon salt

½ teaspoon baking powder

1 teaspoon butter

1 tablespoon Sugar Syrup
(page 248), plus extra for drizzling

2 cups/200 g walnuts,
in pieces (optional)

½ teaspoon ground cinnamon

1 cup/250 g curd (page 249)
or ricotta

Vegetable oil, for deep-frying

Finely crushed pistachios, to serve

Whisk together the flour, yeast, sugar, salt, and baking powder with 1 ½ cups/350 ml lukewarm water to make a pancake batter (if the water is too hot, it kills the yeast; if it's too cold, it won't work). Leave the mixture to rest for 30 minutes.

Grease a frying pan with the butter and set it over high heat. When the pan is hot and the butter has melted, pour a ladle of the pancake mix into the pan (it will undoubtedly go wrong, as the first one always does!). The idea is to make small circular pancakes of around 4 inches/10 cm in diameter and ¼-inch/5 mm thickness. When the pancake heats up, it will bubble and look like an English muffin with holes and a spongy texture. When it has finished bubbling, after a minute or two, it's ready, so take it off the heat and set it aside on a plate, then repeat with the next one. When all the mixture has been used, leave the pancakes to cool.

Mix 1 tablespoon of sugar syrup with the walnuts and cinnamon.

Take a pancake, put a small amount of the nut mixture in the middle and fold it into a half-moon shape. Seal the edges by pressing them together tightly with your fingertips. The spongy texture of the pancakes should naturally stick together; if not, try using a tiny bit of the sugar syrup on it.

Do the same thing if you are using curd or ricotta. You can also stuff the pancakes with both curd and walnuts.

Heat a saucepan filled halfway with vegetable oil over medium-high heat. When the oil is hot, deep-fry the stuffed pancakes until they have turned golden brown. Remove from the oil with a slotted spoon and place on paper towels to drain. When they are all ready and on a tray, generously pour over more sugar syrup, sprinkle with pistachios, and eat immediately.

Butter Cookies
(Ghraibi)

Fatima is naturally creative, and everything she makes looks perfect—every cookie is exactly the same size and shape—and she could, without a doubt, be a professional pastry chef. Fatima and her family hail from one of the worst affected areas in Homs, and they moved to Beirut in 2013. With no work to keep her busy and an urge to do something to pass the time, Fatima took a course in how to run a small business, at the end of that six-week course, each participant had to submit a business proposal. Some women had proposals for sewing projects or hair salons, but Fatima's business idea was to bake pastries at home and sell them to bakeries. She baked these cookies, as well as some incredible stuffed croissants, as part of her presentation and won first prize. With the money she won, she bought a fridge and an oven and hasn't stopped baking since.

When we met her in Beirut, we made these very simple cookies with her in that same little oven.

MAKES 15 PIECES

5 tablespoons/75 g butter

⅔ cup/75 g confectioners' sugar

1 teaspoon rose water

1 teaspoon vanilla extract

1 cup/150 g all-purpose flour

1 egg white

1 tablespoon vegetable oil

15 shelled pistachios

Melt the butter slightly, then mix in the confectioners' sugar with a wooden spoon to form a creamy paste. Add the rose water and vanilla extract and mix, then add the flour, egg white, and oil and knead with your hands for 5 to 10 minutes. If it's too dry, add a little more oil. Leave the dough to rest in the fridge for about 30 minutes.

Preheat the oven to 350°F/180°C and line a baking tray with parchment paper.

Make individual balls out of the dough, each about half the size of a golf ball. Gently press a pistachio on top to flatten it ever so slightly, then place on the baking tray. When all the dough has been used, bake in the oven for 12 minutes—they will change color but only slightly; they should still be white, not golden brown, in color.

These are best eaten on the same day.

Eat and Say Thanks

(Kol wa Shkor)

This is a type of baklava that is famous in Damascus. It is made of very fine phyllo pastry, butter, and any nuts of your choice. The phyllo most commonly available in stores is the thinnest type of phyllo and perfect for this recipe, but if you have an option for thicker or thinner dough, always go for the thinnest sheets, labeled #4 phyllo. If you want to know how it gets its name, serve it to your friends and find out. . . .

MAKES APPROXIMATELY 24 INDIVIDUAL SLICES

1½ cups/150 g ground unsalted pistachios

3 tablespoons Sugar Syrup (page 248), plus extra to drizzle

1½ teaspoons ground cardamom

1½ cups/150 g ground walnuts

1½ teaspoons ground cinnamon

20 phyllo pastry sheets (each 8.3 x 11.7 inches/21 x 30 cm; trim if larger)

5 tablespoons/75 g butter, melted

Preheat the oven to 350°F/180°C. Mix the pistachios with half of the sugar syrup and the cardamom. In a separate bowl, mix the walnuts with the cinnamon and the remaining sugar syrup.

Place 2 layers of pastry on top of each other and brush with a generous amount of the melted butter, then place another 2 sheets on top and brush with more butter. Repeat until you have used 10 sheets.

Sprinkle one of the nut mixtures over the top layer so that all of the pastry is covered and the nuts are evenly spread. Tightly roll the pastry, starting with a long edge, like rolling up a rug. When it is rolled into a log shape, brush the outside with melted butter. Repeat the whole process with the remaining 10 pastry sheets and the other nut mixture.

Cut the rolls into ¾ inch/2 cm slices before baking in the oven for about 15 minutes, until they turn golden brown and slightly crispy. Take out of the oven and drizzle with plenty of sugar syrup to taste.

Leave to cool before serving. These can keep for a week in an airtight container.

Spiced Rice Pudding
(Mhalla)

This is a dessert served to guests who come to see you after giving birth, and it confirms Syrians' deep belief in the ability of spices to heal—ginger and cinnamon in particular. This is the perfect dessert for vegans.

SERVES 8–10

½ cup/100 g granulated sugar, or to taste

2 teaspoons ground cinnamon

½ teaspoon ground ginger

½ cup/100 g aborio rice

Handful of walnuts pieces

1⅓ cups/80 g desiccated coconut, or to taste

Pour 4 cups/1 L of water into a saucepan with the sugar and spices. Bring to a boil, then add the rice and turn the heat down to a simmer. Stir occasionally, and when the rice is thick and creamy take it off the heat. Stir in most of the walnuts and coconut, reserving some of each for the top.

Serve in individual bowls while still warm.

Turmeric Cake

(Sfouf)

Turmeric cake may sound unusual—and it is—but this exotic dessert will be the talk of any dinner party. The spicy aromatic flavors combined with the almonds make a delicious moist cake that lasts for a good few days. If you want a gluten-free option, simply replace the semolina with finely ground polenta. This is kind of the cake version of Itab's mother's turmeric pancakes on page 192, and an easier option if you are cooking for a large number of people.

SERVES 6-8

2¼ cups/250 g ground almonds

1 cup/175 g fine semolina

1½ teaspoons baking powder

2 teaspoons ground turmeric

1 teaspoon aniseed, crushed

1 teaspoon ground cinnamon

1 teaspoon nigella seeds

1 cup plus 6 tablespoons/300 g butter, at room temperature

1 cup/200 g granulated sugar

3 eggs, at room temperature

For the sugar syrup

⅓ cup/80 g granulated sugar

Juice of 1 lemon

⅓ cup/80 g water

Confectioners' sugar, for sprinkling

Handful of chopped pistachios, for sprinkling

Handful of dried rose petals, for sprinkling (optional)

Preheat the oven to 320°F/160°C and line a round, 9-inch/23 cm springform pan with parchment paper.

Mix the almonds, semolina, baking powder, turmeric, aniseed, cinnamon, and nigella seeds together in a large bowl.

Beat the butter and sugar together until pale and fluffy. A food processor works perfectly well for this. Add the eggs, one at a time, incorporating well. If it starts to curdle or looks too runny, simply add a spoonful of the dry ingredients.

Fold in the dry ingredients, then pour the mixture into the pan, level with a spatula, and bake for around 40 minutes, or until a skewer inserted into the middle comes out clean.

While the cake is in the oven, make the sugar syrup. Add the sugar, lemon juice, and water to a pan and simmer until the sugar dissolves. The longer you simmer it, the thicker the syrup will become. Ten minutes should be about right.

Take the cake out of the oven and insert a skewer around the edges; then, while still warm, pour the syrup all over so that it seeps into the cake. Leave to cool, then remove from the pan, sprinkle with confectioners' sugar and pistachios, and rose petals, if using, and serve.

Carrot and Coconut Balls
(Jazariyeh)

This is a sweet from the Syrian coast. *Jazariyeh* comes from the word *jazzer*, which means "carrots." First the carrots are shredded and boiled with sugar, nuts, and spices, then the mixture is traditionally shaped into big pyramids. Each pyramid is flavored with different nuts and different spices. In Syria you can buy jazariyeh by the kilo, but here is a version that can easily be made at home.

MAKES 12–15 BALLS

3 carrots, peeled and diced

6 tablespoons Sugar Syrup (page 248)

⅓ cup/35 g walnuts, coarsely chopped

2 tablespoons/10 g desiccated coconut, plus extra to coat (optional)

½ teaspoon ground nutmeg

Boil the carrots in a pan of water until very soft. Drain the carrots really well until all the water has completely gone, then, using a fork or potato masher, roughly mash. Add the sugar syrup and return the pan to the heat for 10 minutes.

Remove from the heat and mix in the walnuts, coconut, and nutmeg and allow to cool. Once cool, divide the mixture into 12 to 15 pieces and roll into individual balls. You can then roll the balls in coconut if you want them covered in snow!

Turmeric Pancakes

(Lazzaqyat)

This is a traditional dessert from Sweida, mainly made for guests or on big occasions like engagement parties or graduations. It has to be served on a big copper tray and eaten with lots of ghee or butter. The traditional way of making it is to layer big pancakes on top of one other, then pour generous amounts of halva sauce over before cutting into it like a cake. The recipe below is an easier way of making and eating this at home.

MAKES 12–14 PANCAKES

For the pancakes

1½ cups/200 g all-purpose flour

1½ cups/350 ml warm water

1½ teaspoons ground turmeric

½ teaspoon ground cinnamon

¼ teaspoon ground aniseed

½ teaspoon instant yeast

½ teaspoon baking powder

½ teaspoon granulated sugar

Butter, for frying

For the sauce

1 cup/250 ml milk

5 ounces/150 g plain
or pistachio halva

Large handful of crushed pistachios

2 tablespoons nigella seeds

Put all the pancake ingredients into a food processor and blend until it forms a very smooth consistency. Cover the batter, then leave to rest in a warm place for 30 minutes.

Meanwhile, make the sauce by blending the milk and halva together until smooth. Pour into a pan and warm over low heat until it thickens, being careful not to boil it as it will separate. Stir in most of the pistachios, leaving some for decoration.

Make the pancakes by pouring a ladle of the batter onto a hot buttered frying pan and, after a minute or two, turning the pancake so that both sides are cooked through. Place the cooked pancakes on a plate, pour the halva sauce over, and sprinkle with the few remaining pistachios and the nigella seeds to serve. Eat immediately.

Razan

Razan is ambitious and bursting with pride. She is a doer, not one to sit around feeling sorry for herself. She was studying pharmacy in Damascus when the war broke out, but when the bombs got closer, and eventually struck just by her husband's office, they decided to leave. Months later they found themselves in Huddersfield, West Yorkshire.

Four months later, Razan was thinking about ways to support her family—and a lightbulb went on. Razan always ate halloumi cheese for breakfast—she was obsessed—but she noticed it wasn't available all year-round in Yorkshire supermarkets, and when she did find it, it was nowhere near the same quality as back home. Although she had no experience in business, she decided then and there to start making and selling her own halloumi.

Fortunately, in Huddersfield, Razan is surrounded by luscious green fields and plentiful supplies of great-quality milk, so armed with advice from the local job center, a small start-up loan, some second-hand equipment, and help from her engineer husband, she built a factory. Yorkshire Dama Cheese has now won prizes across the world, just three years after Razan arrived in Britain.

Her home is a rented townhouse with bright red kitchen walls and evidence of kids everywhere. Her mother-in-law sat and watched the whole time we were in the kitchen, supervising with an expert's eye. She would join in with the odd conversation about cooking, chipping in to insist on her way of rolling cabbage leaves, which was just a little bit different than Razan's.

We made stuffed cabbage together, put them on the stove to cook, and then went to collect the kids (who all have very strong Yorkshire accents), then went to her factory. We watched them making halloumi, then got to taste it when it had just been boiled—and it was insanely delicious.

The conflict in Syria has taken Razan on a very different path than the one she was on in Damascus, yet it was her ambition and strong love of food that has given her a new chance to build a future for herself and her family.

Stuffed Pastry Parcels
(Namoura)

Razan (see page 194) makes these simple, delicious pastry parcels with the curd they make in their factory in Huddersfield. They are now branching out from the original halloumi and are offering other dairy products made from Yorkshire milk. She told us that people are still not as familiar with products such as labneh or areesha (curd) as they are with halloumi, but hopefully this recipe and others like it will help change that. If you want to make your own curd, see page 249. If you don't have time for that, you can use ricotta instead.

MAKES 20 PIECES

For the filling

1 teaspoon butter, plus extra
for melting

⅔ cup/150 ml milk (if using curd)

¼ cup/50 g granulated sugar
(optional)

1 teaspoon cornstarch mixed
with a drop of water (if using curd)

7 ounces/200 g curd or ricotta

8 ounces/250 g phyllo pastry sheets

For the syrup

½ cup/120 g granulated sugar

½ cup/120 ml water

Crushed pistachios, to serve

Preheat the oven to 350°F/180°C and grease a baking tray with a little butter.

Heat the milk and sugar, if using, in a pan over low heat, stirring continuously, and just before it boils, add the cornstarch and whisk in the curd. If using ricotta, you can skip this heating, and simply stir the sugar into the ricotta. Turn off the heat.

Lay 5 pastry sheets on top of each other and cut them into 2½-inch/6 cm squares or thereabouts. Fill each square with a little of the curd mix, then fold over into a triangle and place on the baking tray. If the corners don't stick, just dab a bit of the curd on them to act as a glue. When your baking tray is full, brush each triangle with a little melted butter and cook the pastry parcels in the oven for approximately 20 minutes.

Meanwhile, make the sugar syrup. Heat the sugar and water in a pan over low heat until all the sugar has dissolved and the syrup has thickened. Leave to cool.

When the pasty parcels have turned a nice golden brown, take them out of the oven and pour the syrup over them immediately. Sprinkle with pistachios.

These are best eaten straight away.

Milk Pudding

(Muhallabiyeh)

This is a very light dessert that is simple, is cheap to make, and can be prepared far in advance, which is our favorite kind of dessert when cooking for a large group.

They say the name of this pudding comes from the Umayyad Prince of Damascus, Al Muhallab Ibn Abi Sufra. One day, the bored potentate ordered his servants to make him something different, a special dessert, and this is what they came up with using the only ingredients they had—milk, sugar, starch, and mastic, which has a sweet, licorice flavor and is now used in many Middle Eastern dishes. Apparently the pudding then became known as the "milk of the princes," but commoners soon caught on to how simple it was to prepare and it became known among them as the "milk of the commons." Nowadays people flavor the milk with a variety of spices, depending on each individual's taste.

This pudding has a smooth texture, with the nuts on top adding a crunch, which Syrians love. This is one of the most ubiquitous desserts in Damascus.

SERVES 12

4 cups/1 L milk

1 cup/200 g granulated sugar

3 tablespoons cornstarch

1 tablespoon rose water
or orange blossom water

½ teaspoon vanilla extract

¼ cup/20 g pistachios, crushed

Dried rose petals, to decorate
(optional)

In a saucepan, gently heat the milk and sugar over low heat, stirring regularly. Mix the cornstarch with a few drops of water, just enough to make a loose, smooth paste. Just before it boils, add the cornstarch mix and stir constantly until it thickens, then add the rose water and vanilla. Once it reaches a nice thick consistency, pour the mixture into individual bowls or trifle glasses and leave to cool.

Once cool, put them in the fridge to set for at least 2 hours.

When you are ready to serve the pudding, sprinkle with the crushed pistachios and, if you want some extra color, dried rose petals.

Bird's Nests
(Osh el Bulbul)

We cooked these quirky little sweet pastries with Samira, whom we met in a refugee camp inside Syria. Samira was a professional pastry caterer from Damascus. When the fighting broke out in their suburbs, she and her husband had to flee quickly. Samira left everything behind apart from her three battered hand-written recipe books. "They are the most precious items in my life," she told us. Samira, despite being petite in appearance, is very strong in nature. She is the bread winner for her family. Even after she moved to a refugee camp, Samira quickly started her own small business, selling her tent-made sweets to fellow refugees. With the money she made, she managed to buy a fridge and a small stove and expand a little.

You only need to look at a picture of Osh el Bulbul to know how these little sweet, crunchy parcels got their name. They are served at weddings a lot. You can make the nests as big or as small as you like; they are the perfect canapé and are actually really fun and very easy to make.

SERVES 6–8

8 ounces/250 g Kadaifi pastry (page 248)

5 tablespoons/75 g butter, melted

1½ cups/150 g shelled pistachios

½ cup/120 ml Sugar Syrup (page 248)

Preheat the oven to 350°F/180°C.

Lay the pastry out on a large clean surface. Cut the pastry strands so that they are about 12 inches/30 cm long—obviously the longer they are, the larger the parcels. Take a few strands of the pastry, wrap them around two fingers, and put in a deep oven tray or cake tin. Repeat until the tray is full and all the pastry nests are packed tightly next to each other, so they stay in place.

Pour the melted butter on top and bake until golden brown and crispy on top—about 10 minutes.

Mix the pistachios with a bit of sugar syrup and leave to one side.

When the nests are done, place 2 to 3 pistachios in each nest, then pour the rest of the sugar syrup over them.

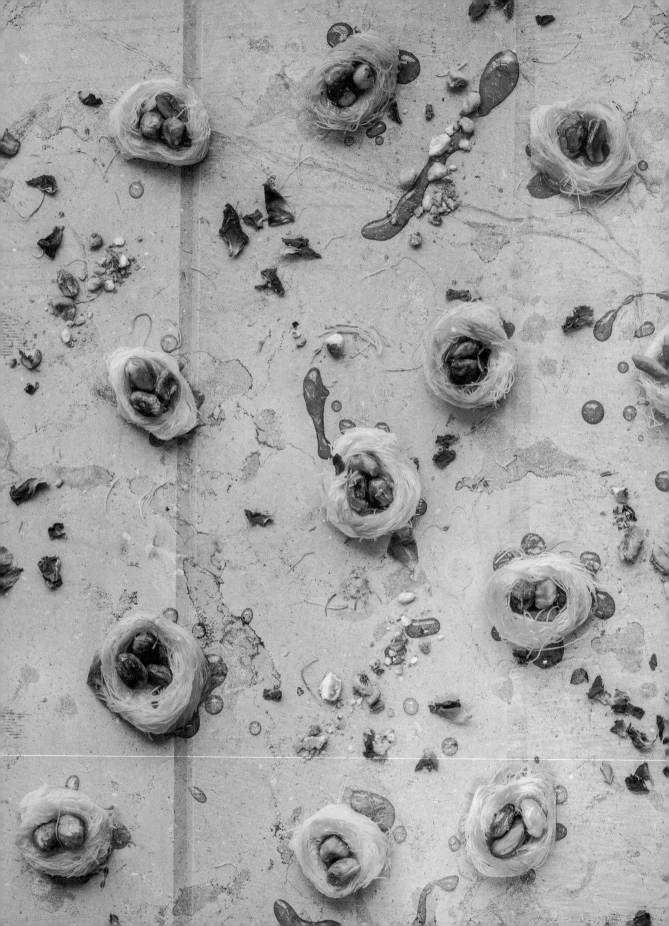

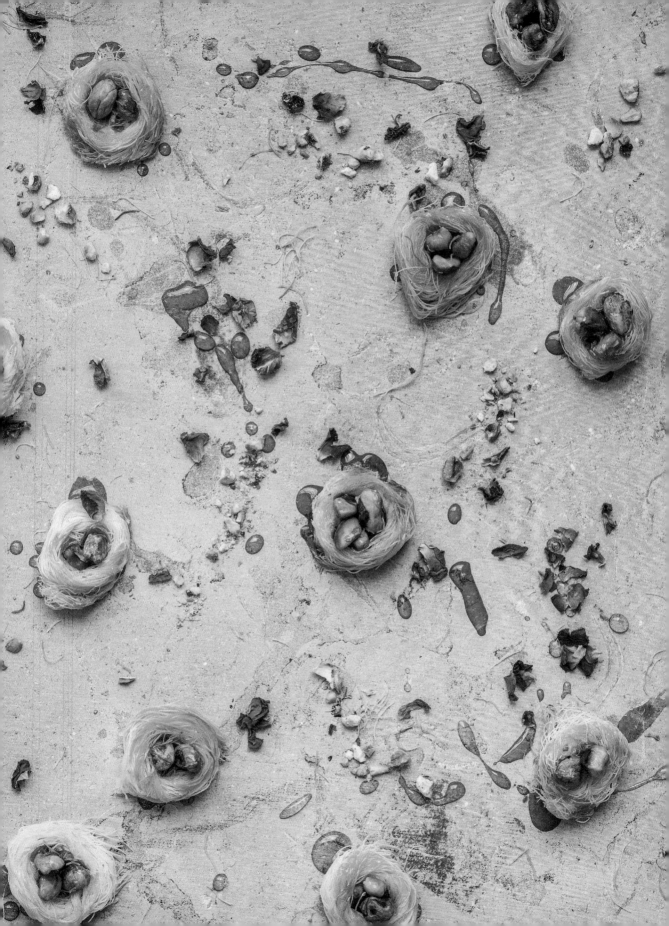

Stuffed Dates

(Tamar Mahshi)

Dates are believed to have originated in Iraq and have been a staple food in the Middle East for thousands of years. During Ramadan, Muslims always break their daily fast with a couple of dates before anything else because the nutrients and natural sugars they hold are believed to be good after so many hours without food or water. It is said that the Prophet Mohammed used to break his fast that way too.

Dates are often given as gifts, for any occasion, and can come in anything from interesting boxes to luxuriously wrapped trays.

This is not so much a traditional recipe as a sensational invention of Razan's (see page 194). When she introduced us to her dates stuffed with tarragon, we couldn't believe the explosion of flavors. The way the clean, cool, aniseed flavor of the tarragon cuts through the sweetness of the dates is amazing. It's hard to imagine it working until you've tried it. We've served them at various supper clubs in London, and they go down incredibly well.

Here is the very simple recipe, which is great served with tea or coffee at the end of the meal.

SERVES 10–12

24 pitted dates
Bunch of fresh tarragon

Stuff the dates with one or two tarragon leaves. It's as simple as that.

Semolina and Coconut Cake

(Harrisi Nabkiyeh)

Nabkan Semolina is a famous dessert throughout Syria. Nabk is an area in the Qalamoun Mountains near the border with Lebanon, and Nabkan Semolina is a dense cake with loads of sugar syrup poured on top. Before the war broke out, anyone with any sense traveling from Damascus to Homs made sure to stop on the way at the most famous semolina cake maker, Al Nabki. This recipe is inspired by those visits, although it is a little spongier and lighter and takes less time to make.

MAKES AROUND 25–35 LITTLE SQUARES

2½ cups/400 g fine semolina

1½ cups/300 g granulated sugar

3 cups/200 g desiccated coconut

2 cups/480 g plain yogurt

2 cups/480 ml whole milk

2 tablespoons baking powder

For the topping

½ cup/100 ml Sugar Syrup (page 248) with 1 teaspoon rose water

Handful of sliced almonds (optional)

Handful of shelled pistachios (optional)

Handful of coconut flakes (optional)

Preheat the oven to 350°F/180°C and line an 8 x 11-inch/ 22 x 30 cm baking pan with parchment paper.

In a large bowl, add the semolina, sugar, coconut, yogurt, and milk and leave to rest for 10 minutes.

Add the baking powder, mix well, then pour into the baking pan. Sprinkle with the nuts, if using, and bake in the oven for 30 to 40 minutes until golden brown.

Make the sugar syrup with a splash of rose water and pour on the cake as soon as it comes out of the oven. Sprinkle on the coconut, if using.

Leave to cool, then cut into 1½-inch/4 cm squares.

Sesame Cookies

(Baraazek)

A common gift from anyone coming back from Damascus is a tin of these thin and crunchy sesame cookies. The Syrian capital is famous for making the best Baraazek; they are the perfect afternoon snack with a glass of cardamom tea, and the great thing about them is they will last for weeks in an airtight container.

MAKES APPROXIMATELY 20 COOKIES

4 tablespoons/60 g butter

¾ cup/120 g all-purpose flour

¼ cup/60 g granulated sugar

¼ teaspoon baking powder

¼ teaspoon vanilla extract

1 egg yolk

½ cup/50 g sesame seeds

1 tablespoon Sugar Syrup (page 248)

½ cup/50 g shelled pistachios, roughly chopped

Preheat the oven to 350°F/180°C and line a baking tray with parchment paper.

Melt the butter so that it is just softer than room temperature but not quite fully liquid.

Combine the butter, flour, sugar, baking powder, vanilla, and egg yolk in a mixing bowl and knead together to form a dough for a good 10 minutes. Leave, covered, for about 15 minutes.

Mix the sesame seeds in a small shallow bowl with the sugar syrup. Fill another shallow bowl with the pistachios.

Take a small amount of dough, roughly the size of a large marble, and roll it into a ball. Flatten it in the palm of your hands to make a very thin, round shape, then press into the sesame seeds. Gently turn it over, then press into the pistachios. Alternatively, you can push a few pistachios into the other side individually. Press the cookie in the palms of your hands again. You should now have a cookie with pistachios on one side and sesame seeds on the other. Repeat with the remaining dough.

Place the cookies on the baking tray, pistachio-side down, and bake in the oven for about 10 minutes, watching them closely until they have slightly changed color. They are very thin so be careful not to burn them. Transfer to a wire rack to cool.

Cookies Stuffed with Dates

(Ma'moul)

In a neighborhood in Sweida, southern Syria, we met Um Mohammed. A bubbly, larger-than-life character, she had fled her home in the Damascus suburbs due to an intensified regime bombardment. Her first priority upon arriving in Sweida was to integrate and make friends, so she rented a flat and decided to accomplish her mission by baking huge amounts of her favorite pastries: Ma'moul. She told us that the smell of cardamom filled the entire building for a good few days after. Um Mohammed knocked on every door in her building and offered her date-filled pastries to all the neighbors. She said, "Since that day I have been friends with all my neighbors, who are all from different religions. My ma'moul saved me." We ordered ma'moul molds online, and found beautiful wooden ones in Syria.

MAKES APPROXIMATELY 30 COOKIES

For the dough

½ cup plus 1 tablespoon/
125 g unsalted butter

2 cups/125 g all-purpose flour

1½ tablespoons/20 ml water

1½ tablespoons/20 ml rose water

¼ cup/50 g granulated sugar

For the filling

1 teaspoon butter

12 ounces/325 g date paste

2 teaspoons ground cardamom, preferably freshly ground

Crushed pistachios or sesame seeds (optional)

For the dough, melt the butter, and mix in flour with a fork. Add the water, rose water, and sugar and knead for 5 to 10 minutes. Leave to rest for 1 hour.

For the filling, heat the butter, date paste, and cardamom in a saucepan. Leave to cool. Once cool enough to handle, make the mixture into 30 little ½-inch/1.5 cm balls.

Preheat the oven to 350°F/180°C and line a baking tray with parchment paper.

When the dough has rested, divide it into small 1-inch/2.5 cm balls and, with your forefinger, make a fairly big hole in each by gently spinning the ball around your finger. The dough should be as thin as possible, without tearing.

Place a date ball in each hole and seal it in by pulling the dough over it. Now place the parcel into the mold, press it down firmly, then tap it out onto the baking tray. If you don't have molds, you can make them into balls by hand, then roll them in sesame seeds or chopped pistachios to coat, if desired.

Bake in the oven for about 20 minutes.

Layered Pastry
(Knafe)

Knafe dates back to thirteenth-century Aleppo and was fit for many a caliph. It has since become a popular dessert all over the Middle East and is, unsurprisingly, sold in sweet shops all around Syria. It is made in a massive tray that has to be positioned over low heat, as it is stuffed with cheese that would go solid if cold. The coarse Knafe itself is made from a very thin noodle-like dough called kadaifi, a bit like shredded wheat. You can find kadaifi pastry in the U.S., mainly in the frozen sections of big Arabic and Turkish shops.

With only four ingredients, Knafe is very easy to make and melts in your mouth.

SERVES 6

10 ounces/300 g Kadaifi pastry (page 248)

½ cup plus 1 tablespoon/125 g butter

7 ounces/200 g fresh mozzarella cheese, roughly torn and completely drained

¾ cup/200 ml Sugar Syrup (page 248) with 1 tablespoon rose water

Handful of shelled pistachios, finely chopped

Preheat the oven to 350°F/180°C and grease an 8- to 9-inch/20 to 23 cm round springform cake pan.

Cut up the pastry so that it is little, short, fine strands and divide into 2 equal piles.

Melt the butter, then pour half into one pile of pastry and mix well with your fingers so that all the pastry is coated. Do the same to the other half. Place one half of the pastry evenly onto the bottom of the pan and press down firmly with your fingers. Spread the cheese on top, leaving a ½-inch/1 cm border from the edge, then top with the second half of the pastry, covering the whole thing and applying a bit of pressure.

Bake in the oven for about 30 minutes, or until it is a lovely golden brown color.

Take it out of the oven, pour on the sugar syrup, and sprinkle over the chopped pistachios. Eat while still warm so the melted cheese oozes out.

Aniseed Cookies

(Baskout El Yansoon)

These little delights are not too sweet, and they go perfectly with afternoon tea or coffee. While writing this book, we always had these in a tin at arm's length; they make a handy little afternoon snack.

MAKES APPROXIMATELY 40 COOKIES

2½ cups/400 g fine semolina

½ cup/50 g granulated sugar

1 teaspoon baking powder

Pinch of salt

¼ cup plus 3 tablespoons/100 g butter, melted

¾ cup/200 ml milk

1 egg, whisked

3 tablespoons ground aniseed

1 tablespoon nigella seeds, plus extra to top

Preheat the oven to 350°F/180°C.

Mix all the dry ingredients, then add the butter and mix with your hands until it is distributed evenly. Pour in the milk and mix well. After the mixture is formed into a dough, make a well in the middle and add the egg, then knead. Add the aniseed and the nigella seeds and mix well.

Divide the dough into little balls. Roll each ball into long strips, then bring the two ends together.

Sprinkle with more nigella seeds, then bake in the oven for 20 minutes, or until they start to turn slightly golden.

Semolina and Halloumi Pudding

(Ma'mouniyeh)

In a camp near Hanover, in Germany, we caught up with Nasreen and her family of 16. They fled Aleppo, where her husband, Tarek, used to run a chain of ful and falafel restaurants, and made their way to Turkey, then crossed the Aegean Sea in a rubber dinghy. For Nasreen and Tarek, cooking Aleppian food is like breathing, but, sadly, in a German camp with no cooking facilities and where electrical items are not allowed, this is impossible. However, like many other refugees, in the face of adversity they find ways to keep Syria in their lives.

Nasreen's kids snuck us and a kettle into their room through the back of the building. There she made us Ma'mouniyeh—in the kettle. Ma'mouniyeh is a delicious hot pudding made with semolina and halloumi cheese, usually cooked in a saucepan (unless you live in a bunker in Germany).

This sweet and salty pudding is eaten in Aleppo on a Friday morning, as a weekend breakfast treat.

SERVES 4

¼ cup/50 g granulated sugar

5 tablespoons/75 g butter

⅓ cup/60 g fine semolina

½ teaspoon ground cinnamon, plus more for sprinkling

3 ounces/80 g halloumi, cut into ½-inch/1 cm cubes

Handful of walnuts pieces (optional)

Heat the sugar and 1⅔ cups/400 ml of water in a saucepan until the sugar dissolves.

Meanwhile, melt the butter in a frying pan, then add the semolina. Fry, and keep stirring until it soaks up all the butter. When it turns a golden brown color, it's ready.

Add the semolina and cinnamon to the sugar water and simmer over low heat for about 5 minutes, stirring constantly.

When the semolina is smooth and thick in consistency, drop the halloumi into it, stir, and serve in bowls sprinkled with cinnamon and nuts on top, if you like.

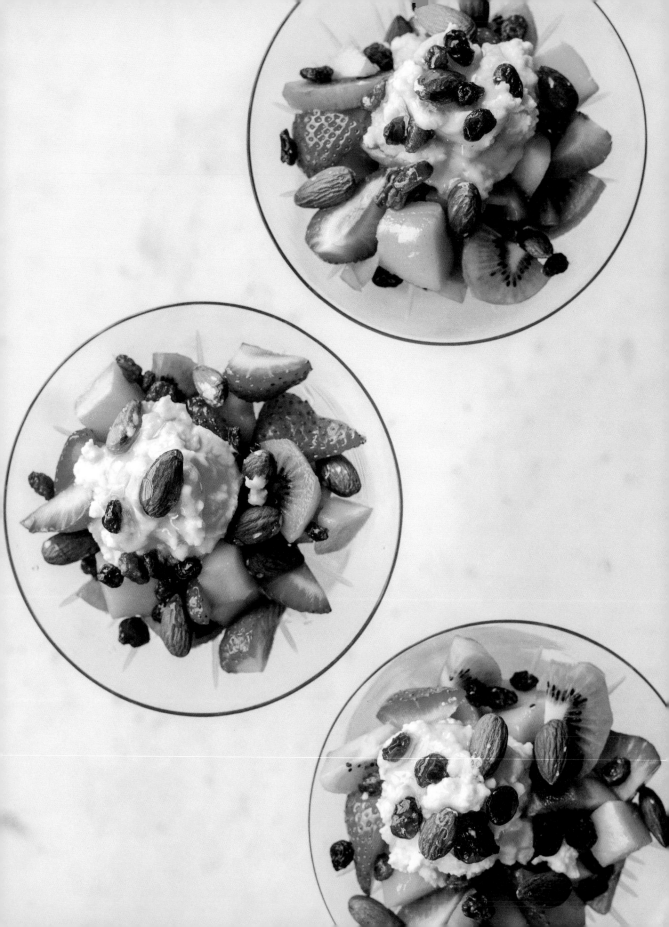

Damascene Fruit Salad

(Salatat Fawakeh)

Abu Shakir is the name of the oldest juice and fruit cocktail bar in Damascus—it is more than 80 years old. Juice bars exist all around the country; they are places where everyday working people can get a hit of ice-cold fresh orange juice squeezed on the spot or a banana smoothie. Groups of friends, students, and giggling school girls sit for hours on little plastic chairs perched on the narrow pavement in front of Abu Shakir's. The best thing about this particular place is that the owner keeps challenging himself to take the smoothie and fruit salad to new levels of elaboration. Sometimes you can get a smoothies tabakat (a colorful array of smoothies layered in complex patterns to form an impressive rainbow effect) with fruit salad and creamy curd on top. In this version we have tried our humble best to emulate the lushness of Abu Shakir.

SERVES 4

8 strawberries, quartered

1 mango, pitted and diced

1 apple, chopped

1 banana, sliced

1 kiwi, sliced

8 ounces/250 g milk curd (page 249) or ricotta

Honey, for drizzling

Handful of whole almonds

Handful of raisins

Toss all the chopped fruit together in a big bowl, then divide among smaller individual bowls.

Put a tablespoon of curd or ricotta onto each serving, drizzle with honey, and sprinkle with nuts and raisins.

Christmas Chocolate Cake

Hala (see page 86) absolutely loves this Christmas season special, and her family calls it "disappearing cake" because, mysteriously, you take it out of the oven near anyone with taste buds and it does exactly that. So dangerous was it to leave within eyesight that her mother had a special hiding place under the fridge, which, needless to say was quickly discovered. "My siblings and I always knew where it was and would sneak in when nobody was there and have a bite."

With this recipe you can't stint on the very particular decoration. Every year Hala's mother would go to the old man's shop that sells everything and buy the decoration for the cake—little colorful Smarties-like sweets—and ever since, that image has become embedded in her mind as the definitive cake. "I have tried French, Italian, and English cakes, but the one in my head is always this one," she admits. Hala hasn't cooked Disappearing Cake since she arrived in England. "I am not ready for the rush of memories just yet."

SERVES 8

1¾ cups/225 g all-purpose flour

1½ cups/325 g granulated sugar

6½ tablespoons unsweetened cocoa powder

1 teaspoon baking powder

1 teaspoon baking soda

3 eggs, beaten

1 teaspoon vanilla extract

Grated zest of 1 orange

1 cup/250 ml milk

¾ cup plus 2 tablespoons/200 ml vegetable oil

⅔ cup/150 ml freshly squeezed orange juice

For the icing

5 ounces/150 g chopped dark or milk chocolate

⅔ cup/150 ml heavy cream

Preheat the oven to 350°F/180°C and line a 9-inch/23 cm round springform cake pan, or a 35 x 30 cm Christmas tree tin, with parchment paper.

Combine the flour, sugar, cocoa, baking powder, and baking soda in one large bowl. In a separate large bowl, beat the eggs with the vanilla and zest, add the milk, vegetable oil, and orange juice, then fold in the dry ingredients.

Transfer to the cake pan and bake in the oven for 40 to 50 minutes, or until a skewer inserted into the middle comes out clean. Tent with foil if the top starts to crack before the center is cooked. Leave to cool in the pan, then turn the cake onto a wire rack to cool completely.

For the icing, melt the chocolate and the cream in a saucepan over low heat. Whisk very well and set aside to cool and thicken for around half an hour. Once it is thick, spread over the cooled cake and decorate as you wish.

Drinks

Amidst the dust and sweat of a Middle Eastern summer, everyone is perennially gasping for refreshment, and so an unrivaled culture of innovation has thrived for centuries when it comes to soft drinks.

From the man with a large pot selling cold tamarind drinks to the bottled ayran drinks you can buy from most street stalls and restaurants to hot spicy teas and freshly squeezed juices, Syria has a special knack for non-alcoholic drinks. In the scorching heat, summer lines form in front of every juice bar, and when it's freezing cold, people huddle in cafés for a hot cup of tea with mint.

Ginger and Cinnamon Tea

(Maghli)

It is believed that the spices and walnuts in this drink will purify your blood and accelerate the recovery process after giving birth. Traditionally, it is given to new mothers and all the guests she receives for 40 days after she gives birth. Neither of us has yet given birth, but we love this comforting spicy tea anyway and drank it a lot while writing this book.

SERVES 2

6 cinnamon sticks

1 ounce/20 g dried ginger slices

4 teaspoons ground cinnamon

1 tablespoon/5 g aniseed

Walnuts, chopped, to serve

Honey or sugar, to taste (optional)

Combine 2 cups/500 ml of water in a saucepan with the cinnamon sticks, ginger, cinnamon, and aniseed and boil for 10 minutes.

Strain the liquid and add the walnuts and honey or sugar, if using. If you don't like "bits" in your tea, you could always leave the walnuts whole and serve them on the side.

Salty Yogurt Drink

(Ayran)

Ayran is a savory yogurt and water drink. It's a bit of a change for some Western palates, but it is the number-one go-to refreshing drink on a hot day in the Middle East. It is sold bottled in every shop across the region, and it is an essential accompaniment to a falafel wrap or Syrian omelette. It's really easy to make at home and is best consumed cold.

SERVES 3

¼ cup/4 tablespoons plain yogurt

Salt, to taste

3½ cups/800 ml water

Ice, to serve (optional)

Put the yogurt and salt in a blender and, as you blend, add water until it has a watery consistency. Serve with ice if you want that immediate chill, or make sure the yogurt is already cold.

Lemon and Mint Drink
(Bolo)

Syrians can't get enough of this incredibly refreshing thirst-quencher, especially on a scorching-hot summer day. We wondered where the name comes from, because "bolo" doesn't mean anything in Arabic, and after a lot of research we were surprised to discover that it is actually supposed to be called Polo, not Bolo, after the famous mints with a hole. However, because the Arabic alphabet doesn't have the letter "p," Arabs mostly pronounce a "p" as a "b." Whether it's Bolo or Polo, it's still seriously refreshing.

SERVES 4

3 unwaxed lemons
1¼ cups/300 ml water
⅓ cup/60 g granulated sugar
1 small bunch of fresh mint leaves
4 to 5 ice cubes

Squeeze 2½ of the lemons into a blender. Cut the remaining lemon half in half (leaving skin on). Remove any seeds and add it to the juice and blend. Add the water, sugar, and mint (reserving a sprig for garnish) and blend very well. Add ice cubes, and blend again.

Pour the drink into a short glass, over ice, and serve with a sprig of mint.

Hibiscus Iced Tea

(Shai Karkadi)

Hibiscus flowers were traditionally used as a medicine. They're full of vitamin C and antioxidants and are said to lower blood pressure. On top of that, this tea tastes great—and that's all the reason we need to share the recipe with you.

This can be enjoyed as hot tea or iced. You could even add a bit of vodka to make it a cocktail.

SERVES 4

2 tablespoons dried hibiscus flowers
2 tablespoons honey
3 cups/750 ml boiling water
Ice cubes, to serve
Fresh mint, to serve

Put the flowers and honey in a measuring pitcher, pour in the boiling water, and leave to cool.

Strain the drink, discarding all the flowers, and serve the tea over ice with a sprig of fresh mint.

Sweet Tamarind

(Tamarhindi)

The word "tamarind" comes from Arabic *tamir hindi*, which means "Indian dates." It came to the English language via Arabic and then Latin. The tamarind drink is a must for Ramadan, but it is also usually sold by men dressed in traditional gear holding a massive flower pot on their backs, who wander around markets clinking their glasses to draw attention.

SERVES 2

1 tablespoon tamarind paste
1 tablespoon rose water
2 tablespoons granulated sugar
Ice cubes, to serve

Mix the tamarind paste, rose water, and sugar with 1¼ cups/300 ml of cold water. Stir and serve with ice.

Aniseed Tea

(Shai Yansoon)

This is a drink that we give to babies in Syria. It is believed to calm them down and help them sleep. It is usually accompanied by aniseed cookies (page 215), or just drunk as an herbal tea in the evening to help one unwind.

MAKES 2 MUGS

½ **cup/50 g aniseed**
2½ **cups/600 ml boiling water**
Honey, to serve (optional)

Put the aniseed in a tea pot or coffee press, add the boiling water, and leave to brew for 5 minutes. Serve with honey, if you wish. If you're serving it to your restless baby, cool it first and leave out the honey for very young ones.

Hot Cumin and Lemon

(Kamoon wa Hamuth)

Cumin is one of the oldest ingredients in the world that we know of. The word comes from the ancient Sumerian "gamun." In Syria people give babies cumin to drink on a regular basis, as they believe it relieves the build-up of gases that result from drinking milk. This cumin drink is an acquired taste, and it might take you a bit of time to get used to it, but try it whenever you have an uneasy tummy.

SERVES 1

Juice of ½ lemon
¼ **teaspoon ground cumin, or to taste**

Fill a mug with boiling water and add the lemon juice and cumin.

Jams & Pickles

An essential beat in the rhythm of Syrian life is the week during summer spent working on jams and pickles to store for the rest of the year. It is a ritual that marks the passing of the seasons as much as any religious festival. In most villages there's no way to wriggle out of rolling your sleeves up the week that Makdous is made. You can't look your neighbor in the eye if you haven't pickled your own olives and made your own tomato paste. Itab remembers when she was a child how her mother always made her and her brother pitch in, and they'd end up with dozens of pounds of Makdous. They would sit around the piles of eggplants and pretend that salting them was a game. One of her earliest, most vivid memories is of picking olives for her parents to make olive oil.

Pickled Turnips and Beets
(Mkhalal Lift wa Shawander)

These delicious crunchy turnips brighten up any mezze. They are perfect as an accompaniment to any meal, in a falafel wrap, or simply on their own.

We use the same amount of beets as turnips here, which gives a darker color, but you can use fewer beets and more turnips to make it a lighter pink if you prefer.

MAKES 1 (1-QUART/1 L) JAR

2 medium turnips

2 medium beets

1½ heaped tablespoons salt

½ cup/125 ml apple cider vinegar (we used unfiltered vinegar for added nutrients)

1⅔ cups/400 ml water

Wash and scrub the turnips and beets really well, cut into quarters or small, bite-sized chunks, and pack into a clean, sterilized jar.

Stir the salt and vinegar with the water until the salt has dissolved, then pour this into the jar until the turnips and beets are completely covered. Seal the jar tightly and store in a cool dark cupboard.

The pickles should be ready in a week and will be bright pink. Once you have opened the jar, keep it refrigerated, and they will last for several weeks.

Fig Jam

(Mrabbat Teen)

The smell of figs bubbling away with aniseed is definitely the scent that most transports us back in time. In the summer, hardly any rooftop in the countryside would be without a thin spread of fig jam slowly drying in the sun. The secret ingredient in Middle Eastern jam-making is the sun, which gives it an incredibly deep, intense flavor.

MAKES 2 (8-OUNCE/250 ML) JARS

1 cup/200 g granulated sugar

4 cups/1 L water

A squeeze of lemon juice

1 pound/500 g fresh figs, stalks removed and finely chopped

2 tablespoons sesame seeds, toasted

Pinch of aniseed

2 tablespoons pine nuts, toasted (optional)

In a saucepan, dissolve the sugar in the water and add the lemon juice. Bring to a boil. Add the chopped figs and leave to simmer over low heat for 1 hour, or until the water has completely evaporated and the jam is thick, stirring regularly.

Mix in the sesame seeds, aniseed, and pine nuts, if using. Pour into sterilized jars when cool. This will keep in the fridge for a month.

Eggplant Jam

Eggplants grow all over Syria in a bewildering array of shapes, colors, and sizes. They are so utterly beloved by everyone in the country that they are eaten in some form for every meal—Syrians will breakfast, lunch, and dine on this king of vegetables; they will eat them pickled, smoked, stuffed, or preserved.

The traditional recipe consists of whole mini eggplants, cored and treated with a food-grade lime powder, which keeps the vegetables firm after cooking. This version, that Majdoleen makes, is much less complex and retains most of the joy and taste of the original, with half the hassle.

MAKES 2 (8-OUNCE/250 ML) JARS

1¼ cups/250 g granulated sugar

8 cups/2 L water

A squeeze of lemon

1 pound/500 g eggplant, peeled and finely diced

6 cloves

Handful of walnuts pieces

Heat the sugar, water, and lemon juice in a large saucepan until the sugar has dissolved.

Add the eggplant and cloves and simmer over low heat until the liquid has thickened and the eggplants have reduced down and formed a nice thick consistency. Take the pan off the heat, mix in the walnuts, and transfer everything to clean sterilized jars, then seal with lids.

This will keep in the fridge for well over a month.

Pickled Cucumbers

Never has a meal we shared with Syrian women been lacking in pickles. Syrians believe that pickles are essential to whet the appetite, cleanse your palate, and provide a sharp, acidic counterpoint to all the rich, oily, and yogurt-y dishes on the menu.

MAKES 1 (1-QUART/1 L) JAR

2 pounds/1 kg baby cucumbers

4 tablespoons salt

1 cup plus 2 tablespoons/275 ml apple cider vinegar (we used unfiltered vinegar for added nutrients)

4 cups/1 L water

Wash the cucumbers and pack into a clean, sterilized jar.

Combine the salt and vinegar with the water, stirring until the salt has dissolved, then pour this into the jar until the cucumbers are completely covered. Seal the jar tightly and store in a cool dark cupboard.

The pickles should be ready in a week. Once you have opened the jar, keep refrigerated, and they will last for several weeks.

Syrian Pantry

For some of the recipes in this book, you'll need an array of ingredients not usually found in kitchens outside the Middle East, so we thought we'd include this as a kind of glossary, a tour of the typical Syrian pantry, dairy products, spice mixes, and more. Some of them you can buy in shops; others you can make yourself and store for a rainy day.

Red Pepper Paste (Dibis Flefle)

This is a paste made by drying red peppers and chiles in the sun, then grinding them and mixing with olive oil to create a thick dark red paste. In Syria you can buy this paste hot, medium, or sweet, depending on how much chile it contains. In the U.S. you can find it in Arab or Turkish supermarkets packed in jars. It can be used like tomato paste to thicken dips, stews, marinades, or just spread on bread with labneh and dried mint.

We don't have the heat in the U.K. to be able to sun-dry our own peppers, but we found that slow-roasting them in the oven works well enough.

MAKES SCANT 1 CUP/200 ML

10 Romano peppers, cut in half and seeded (substitiute red bell peppers)

4 red cayenne or birdseye chiles (if you like it hotter, add more)

5 tablespoons extra-virgin olive oil

Salt, to taste

Preheat the oven to its lowest setting.

Place the peppers and chiles on a sheet pan and roast in the oven for 8 hours. Turn the oven off and leave the peppers in the oven overnight so that they really dry out.

The next day, blend the peppers, chiles, oil, and salt in a food processor and store in a jar in the fridge.

Pomegranate Molasses (Dibis Rumaan)

An absolutely essential item in your Syrian pantry! Made from reducing the juice of a sour variety of pomegranates, this thick, dark syrup is used in almost every dish: sweet or savory. Nowadays you can buy molasses in most mainstream supermarkets, but if not, any Middle Eastern shop will sell it. Make sure you find a brand that uses 100% pomegranate juice with no added sugar.

Tahini

Tahini in Arabic means "to be ground," and so tahini paste is a condiment made from toasted, hulled, ground sesame seeds and nothing else. Most famously used in making hummus, tahini can also be used in sauces, dips, or even desserts, and is widely used all over the Middle East. You can buy it in almost any mainstream supermarket or local shop.

Tahini Sauce

This sauce manages to find its way into a large number of Syrian dishes. You could drizzle any vegetable or meat with it to instantly create a delicacy.

MAKES 6 TABLESPOONS

1 garlic clove
½ teaspoon sea salt
4 tablespoons tahini
Juice of 1 lemon
2 tablespoons plain yogurt
Black pepper, to taste

Using a pestle and mortar, smash the garlic and salt together to form a paste. Add the tahini and lemon juice and stir. The tahini will eventually form a thick, dry texture—don't worry, this is normal. Run your sink faucet very gently and bit by bit add water; keep stirring until the sauce becomes smooth but not too runny.

Add the yogurt and stir. If you prefer a vegan option, simply leave this step out.

Season with pepper (and more salt if needed). You can keep it in the fridge for a few days.

Aleppo Pepper

Aleppo peppers are a type of capsicum that are dried, ground, or crushed and used as spice in Syrian cooking. Like the red pepper paste, you can also buy ground Aleppian pepper sweet, medium, or hot, depending on whether it is made with sweet peppers or chiles. The whole peppers or chiles are salted and dried, then flaked and rubbed with oil, resulting in a wonderfully bright, rich color and delicious sweet flavor. You can buy this online or in certain Arab/Turkish supermarkets in the U.S. If you can't find it, you can use dried chile flakes instead.

7 Spices (7 Baharat)

Baharat means "spices" in Arabic and, as the name suggests, it is a blend of seven different spices. It is used a lot in Syrian cooking, especially with meat dishes. You will be able to find it in some mainstream supermarkets, but if you're an avid cook and have all the spices in your cupboard already, you might as well mix your own. It's ever so simple.

MAKES 6 TABLESPOONS

1 tablespoon ground cardamom
1 tablespoon ground cinnamon
1 tablespoon ground cumin
1 tablespoon ground coriander
1 tablespoon ground black pepper
½ tablespoon ground cloves
½ tablespoon ground nutmeg

Mix all the spices together and store in a sealable jar.

Sumac

Crushed berries from the sumac shrub give this spice its musty lemony flavor and dark red color. In Syria it is used in salads, or kibbeh or with chicken or lamb. It's readily available in all Middle Eastern shops or supermarkets.

Za'atar

A versatile spice blend. In addition to the dried thyme, sumac, and sesame seeds found in Jordanian, Lebanese, and Palestinian za'atar, the Syrian version has ground roasted chickpeas, fennel seeds, coriander, cumin, black sunflower seeds, and pistachios. It goes particularly well with lamb, but in Syria it is mostly eaten with olive oil and bread. It has become increasingly popular in the U.S. and can be found in many supermarkets now.

Mloukhia

A commonly used leaf found in North Africa and the Middle East, mloukhia is known as jute leaves or West African sorrel in English. The leaves are mostly used fresh in Syria, to make soups and stews, but you can find dried ones in some Arabic specialty shops. When boiled, mloukhia has a slightly thicker texture.

Ghee (Semneh)

Ghee is a type of clarified butter, often misconstrued as being terribly unhealthy when actually it is just a purer form of fat. It is made by melting butter and skimming the fat off the top, separating the solids to leave a yellow liquid when hot that becomes a yellow creamy paste when it has cooled down. You can buy ghee made from vegetable oils if you are vegan, or as a slightly cheaper option.

Bulgur

Bulgur is a whole wheat that has been boiled for a short while, then dried and ground, either coarsely or finely. It has a light, nutty flavor and is eaten a lot in Syria, quite often with Angel Hair Noodles (see below) as a substitute for rice. Fine bulgur is an essential ingredient in Tabbouleh (page 60) and is the main ingredient in most kibbeh.

SERVES 4–6

1½ cups/300 g coarse bulgur wheat, rinsed

1 teaspoon butter

2 ounces/50 g angel hair/vermicelli noodles (optional)

2 cups/500 ml vegetable stock

Salt, to taste

Rinse the bulgur a couple of times and drain.

Melt the butter in a saucepan and fry the noodles, if using for a couple of minutes until they start to turn brown.

Add the bulgur and stir so it's coated in butter and mixed with the noodles.

Add just enough stock to cover the bulgur, bring to a boil and add some salt. Turn the heat down and simmer with a lid on until all the water has evaporated.

Sha'aria (Angel Hair Noodles)

Noodles are obviously not traditionally Arabic, but fine vermicelli noodles have made their way into specific dishes. Most typically in Syria they are fried and cooked with rice or bulgur (see recipe above); you can also add them to soups or lentils for more texture.

Freekeh

Freekeh is an ancient superfood—a durum wheat that has been harvested while still young and green in color. It is then roasted by burning the straw and chaff underneath the piles of freekeh rather than the seeds themselves, which results in a wonderfully aromatic, smoked, green cracked wheat. It gives a lovely depth and hint of smokiness when added to soups or stews but can also be a good substitute for rice.

Vegetable/Chicken Stock

There are some recipes you can get away with using a stock cube for, but others—particularly the rice dishes—rely on the flavors of this homemade stock. This recipe came from Rana, whom we met in the Shatila camp.

To make it vegetarian, simply omit the chicken.

MAKES 4 CUPS/1 L

Any leftover bits of chicken meat/bones

1 onion, quartered

2 small tomatoes, halved

1 dried lime

½ bulb of garlic, whole and unpeeled

1 piece of lemon rind

5 cardamom pods

5 cloves

1 cinnamon stick

¼ teaspoon ground ginger

¼ teaspoon ground turmeric

½ teaspoon 7 spices (page 244)

1 teaspoon salt

½ teaspoon peppercorns

Vegetable oil, for frying

Fry all the ingredients in a pan with some vegetable oil for 2 to 3 minutes until aromatic. If making a chicken stock, fry the chicken with the rest of the ingredients now and leave to boil in the water.

Add 4 cups/1 L of water and bring to a boil, then turn the heat down and leave to simmer for about an hour or so.

Strain through a sieve and remove and discard all the solids. The stock is now ready to use or can be frozen.

Halawa (Halva)

A dry, crumbly sweet that is made from sesame paste (tahini) and sugar. There are many different kinds of halva, such as pistachio, chocolate, honey, vanilla, or, of course, the plain one. It can be eaten as it is or used in desserts.

Semolina

Semolina is ground durum wheat used in making pasta, breakfast cereals, and desserts. It is used a lot in Syrian desserts and keeps well, so it's always handy to have a jar of fine and coarse semolina in your cupboards.

Rose Water

A must-have in your baking cupboard, rose water is essential in Syrian desserts. It is made by distilling rose petals and used in many sweets and desserts. You can easily find bottles of it in any Middle Eastern shop and many supermarkets. It's worth getting a good-quality rose water rather than water that is "flavored with rose."

Sugar Syrup

Sugar syrup is key in Syrian sweets, often poured on top of them instead of using sugar in the actual recipe. It's extremely simple to make: you boil water, sugar, and a squeeze of lemon juice until it turns into a nice thick clear syrup. You can also add a drop of rose water if you want. Here is a recipe that makes about ½ cup/ 100 ml of syrup, but if you want more, just use the same proportion of sugar to water.

½ cup/100 g granulated sugar
½ cup/100 ml water
Squeeze of lemon juice

Bring all the ingredients to a boil, then turn the heat down and simmer until it thickens. The longer you leave it simmering, the thicker it will get. It will also thicken after you turn the heat off, so be careful not to let it thicken too much while still simmering. It should be a bit runnier than honey when you take it off the heat.

Kadaifi Pastry

You can't make this thin, noodle-like, shredded pastry at home because you need a special machine, but you will find it in the frozen section of almost any Arabic or Turkish supermarket. Kadaifi pastry is probably most famously known for being used in Knafe (page 212) but is used in other sweets too.

Date Paste

This is basically pitted, mashed-up dates in a packet. You could pit and mash your own, but it doesn't work out any cheaper or more rewarding, so you might as well save yourself the labor. It is used in sweets such as ma'moul (page 211), or can be mixed with a little cardamom, rolled into balls, and eaten as is. Most Middle Eastern shops will stock it.

Milk Curd (Areesha)

You may not normally think to make your own curd at home, but it is actually incredibly easy. Add salt, nigella seeds, and sesame seeds, and you get Syrian areesha cheese. Add honey and you have a dessert. Leave it without either salt or sugar and it's curd. It takes minutes to make and can be eaten in many desserts, with granola, or spread on toast with date syrup drizzled on top. We love it. One thing to bear in mind is that the amount of curd made is considerably less than the amount of milk you start off with.

MAKES 7 OUNCES/200 G

8 cups/2 L whole milk
Sugar or salt, to taste (optional)
Juice of ½ lemon

Gently heat the milk in a saucepan with the sugar or salt, if using, stirring regularly.

Just before it boils, add the lemon juice and don't stir. It will immediately separate and curdle. With a slotted spoon, scoop out the curd and put it into a sieve or colander lined with cheesecloth to drain. Keep scooping out bits of the curd until there is nothing but the whey left in the pan.

Leave the curd to drain properly for an hour or so, then it's ready to use or can be frozen.

Index

Note: Page references in *italics* indicate photographs.

Grains. *See* Bulgur; Freekeh; Rice
Green Bean(s)
    in Olive Oil, 42, *43*
    and Tomato Stew with Rice, *118,* 119
Greens. *See* Chard; Spinach

H

Halawa (Halva)
    about, 247
    Turmeric Pancakes, 192, *193*
Hibiscus Iced Tea, 228, *229*
Hummus with Meat, *30,* 31

J

Jams
    Eggplant, *238,* 238–39
    Fig, 236, *237*
Jute Leaf Soup, *104,* 105
Jute leaves, about, 245

K

Kadaifi pastry, 248
    Bird's Nests, 200, *202*
    Layered Pastry, 212, *213*

L

Labneh (Strained Yogurt), 56, *57*
    Stuffed Pastries, *76,* 76–77
    Wrap, 89, *90*
Lamb
    Cherry Kebab, 150, *151*
    and Eggplant Kebabs, 166, *167*
    Freekeh Soup, *96,* 97
    Ground, Baba Ganoush with, 142, *143*
    Hummus with Meat, *30,* 31
    Kibbeh in Tray, *156,* 156–57
    Meatballs in a Tomato and Pepper Stew,
        164, *165*
    Mixed Grill, 160–61, *162–63*
    and Okra Stew, 154, *155*
    Old Man's Ears, 146–48, *149*
    and Peas, Rice with, *168,* 169
    Stuffed Eggplant, 110, *111*
    The Stuffed Sheikh, *140,* 141
    and White Bean Stew, 170, *171*
Lemon
    and Cumin, Hot, 230, *231*
    and Mint Drink, *226,* 227

Lentil(s)
    Brown, and Bulgur, *112,* 113
    Burnt Fingers, 114–16, *117*
    and Chard Soup, *100,* 101
    Red, Kibbeh, 26, *27*
    Red, Soup, 99

M

Meatballs in a Tomato and Pepper Stew,
    164, *165*
Milk curd. *See* Curd
Milk Pudding, *198,* 199
Mint
    and Cabbage Salad, *54,* 55
    and Garlic, Zucchini with, 36, 37
    and Lemon Drink, *226,* 227
    Tabbouleh, *25,* 60
Mloukhia
    about, 245
    Jute Leaf Soup, *104,* 105

N

Nuts. *See* Almonds; Pine nuts; Pistachios;
    Walnut(s)

O

Okra and Lamb Stew, 154, *155*
Olives, Spiced, 56, *57*
Omelette, Syrian, 80, *81*
Onions
    Brown Lentils and Bulgur, *112,* 113
    Burnt Fingers, 114–16, *117*
    Caramelized, and Sumac, Chicken with,
        124, *125*
    The Fisherman's Catch, *176,* 176–77

P

Pancakes
    Sweet Stuffed, *182,* 182–83
    Turmeric, 192, *193*
Parsley
    Falafel Wrap, *82,* 82–83
    Stuffed Pastries, *76,* 76–77
    Syrian Omelette, 80, *81*
    Tabbouleh, *25,* 60
Pastries, Stuffed, *76,* 76–77

Acknowledgments

First and foremost we would deeply like to thank the Syrian women we have got ten to know over these last two years, who have welcomed us with open arms and shared their kitchens, recipes, and stories with love: Ahlam, Dzovik, Fatima, Fedwa, Hala, Israa', Khouloud, Majdoleen, Mona, Montaha, Nour, Rana, Razan, Reem, Salha, Samira, Shaima, Taghrid, Tahani, Um Mohammed, and Zarifa.

Huge thanks to Bea Hemming for her passion, commitment, and encouragement. You completely believed in us, the recipes, and the stories we collected. We were sad to see you leave but very grateful for introducing us to the wonderfully enthusiastic Anna Valentine. How lucky we were to have had two publishers to guide us along the way.

To Jack MacInnes, our rock! Your passion, enthusiasm, support, help, and, of course, taste buds have been valuable from day one. We couldn't have done it without you.

Our dear friend Hal Scardino for pretty much everything—advice, help, laughs, continued support, allowing us to use your amazing flat for photoshoots and supper clubs. Hal, we love you and are eternally grateful for having you share our journey.

Itab's mother, Dunia, and aunty Nawal, who are still in Syria and who have not only been a source of strength and encouragement throughout, but are incredible cooks and have always been there at the end of a WhatsApp message for a last-minute recipe consultation.

We are so grateful to our friends and photographers Suzannah Baker-Smith and Tabitha Ross for joining us in the refugee camps of Beirut to capture those precious moments. And to Hassan Kattan for photographing life among the destruction of Aleppo.

The Orion team who made our photoshoots such fun—photographers Liz and Max Haraala Hamilton, stylist Maud Eden, and designer Steve Marking. Thanks for your wonderful dedication and commitment.

Big thank you to our friends Dan Gorman, Yasmin Fedda, Julian Johnson, Rania Aboud, and Park Road Kitchen for your constant support and for letting us test recipes in your kitchens.

Aline Kamakian, thank you for allowing us into the kitchen of your wonderful Armenian restaurant, Mayrig in Beirut. Bob Miller and Judy Wilber, thank you for enthusiastically testing recipes all the way from San Francisco. To all at Complicite, you guys are ace—thanks for all your support.

Finally, we'd like to say a big thank you to those closest to us who are constantly there lending their support—Mamdouh Azzam, Tammam and Feras Azzam, Fedaa Al Qaq, Manya Elendary, Maria and Mohammed Mousawi, Nadya, Sam, and Nabeel Mousawi, Bridgette Auger, Manaf and Raghad, Lindsey and Ian MacInnes, and of course, Jim Sturgess.

Note on charity

The authors have donated part of their advance for this book to the Hands Up Foundation.

Hands Up is an innovative charity that was set up by four British friends. United by a sense of sadness at the unfolding crisis in Syria and inspired by their time in Damascus, they wanted to remind their friends in Syria that they had not been forgotten. Now a U.K. registered charity, Hands Up raises money and awareness through creative fundraising

initiatives in the U.K., including the Syrian Supper Club, MarmalAid, and Singing for Syrians.

With their partner organizations working in and around Syria, they identify projects that will have maximum impact for those in need. Where possible this work is inside Syria and run by Syrians. To date Hands Up has supported the salaries of medical staff, winterization projects, and a prosthetic limb clinic.

The aid is direct and designed to support Syrians who will one day have the chance to rebuild their country.

The authors met many of the women through Open Art Foundation. Please support at www.openartfoundation.org.